ISLAMIC |

MW00930905

(NIKAH) A TO Z GUIDE AND MASAIL FAQ

ALL EXPLANATION ABOUT MARRIAGE AND MASAIL IN THE LIGHT OF HADITH AND QURANIC VERSES

Published By: The Way of Islam, 6 Cave Street, Preston, Lancashire, PR1 4SP

Contents

Marriage without Wali (consent)?

"[24:32] Arrange the marriage of the spouseless among you, and the capable from among your bondmen and bondwomen. If they are poor, Allah will enrich them out of His grace. Allah is All-Encompassing, All-Knowing."

Caution:

This article is not to provide justification for our Sisters to get married without the permission and consent of their Wali (guardian). Rather, we advise Sisters who have Wali (guardian) unreasonably preventing them from fulfilling half of their religion to refer the matter to Islamic Scholars or Islamic Shariah councils and let a Mufti or a Scholar from a Shariah council and let them consider the situation and act as Wali (if necessary) and give them in marriage.

This purpose of this article is demonstrated academically that some leeway in the Hanafi School of thought on the matter of marriage without wali (consent) is not without evidence. Due to the sensitivity of the subject, we advise (again) that although leeway does exist our Sisters should opt to consult Islamic Scholars on the matter and let them rule on their individual circumstances and act as their Wali.

Please proceed to read the evidence of the Hanafi School of thought once you have understood the position and the rationale behind this article. Following are some contacts for our Sisters to consult Islamic Scholars and have the Ulama rule on their individual circumstances and assist (if necessary); at the very least local Imam (or local Mosque) should be consulted. Nikah should be publicised and officially endorsed, **please also read out detailed article on marriages**.

Islamic Tarbiyah Academy (UK)

Birmingham Fiqh Council (UK)

Rahmat-e-Alam Foundation (Chicago, USA)

Shariah Board of New York (USA) [redirect through above site)

Fatwa Centre of America (Rhode Island, USA)

Darul Qasim (Chicago, USA)

Evidence for marriage without wali (consent):

Qur'aan encourages believers to marry without placing any restrictions on a believing woman needing a Wali.

وَأَنكِحُوا۟ ٱلْأَيَـٰمَىٰ مِنكُمْ وَٱلصَّـٰلِحِينَ مِنْ عِبَادِكُمْ وَإِمَآئِكُمْ ۚ إِن يَكُونُوا۟ فُقَرَآءَ يُغْنِهِمُ ٱللَّهُ مِن فَضْلِهِۦ ۗ وَٱللَّهُ وَٰسِعٌ عَلِيمٌ

[24:32] Arrange the marriage of the spouseless among you, and the capable from among your bondmen and bondwomen. If they are poor, Allah will enrich them out of His grace. Allah is All-Encompassing, All-Knowing.

There is no question about a woman who is divorced or widowed and her ability to marry without the permission of her Wali.

وَإِذَا طَلَّقْتُمُ ٱلنِّسَآءَ فَبَلَغْنَ أَجَلَهُنَّ فَلَا تَعْضُلُوهُنَّ أَن يَنكِحْنَ أَزْوَٰجَهُنَّ إِذَا تَرَٰضَوْا۟ بَيْنَهُم بِٱلْمَعْرُوفِ ۗ ذَٰلِكَ يُوعَظُ بِهِۦ مَن كَانَ مِنكُمْ يُؤْمِنُ بِٱللَّهِ وَٱلْيَوْمِ ٱلْءَاخِرِ ۗ ذَٰلِكُمْ أَزْكَىٰ لَكُمْ وَأَطْهَرُ ۗ وَٱللَّهُ يَعْلَمُ وَأَنتُمْ لَا تَعْلَمُونَ

[2:232] When you have divorced women, and they have reached (the end of) their waiting period, do not prevent them from marrying their husbands when they mutually agree with fairness.

4

Thus the advice is given to everyone of you who believes in Allah and in the Hereafter. This is more pure and clean for you. Allah knows and you do not know.

حَدَّثَنِي مَعْقِل بْن يَسَار قَالَ : كَانَتْ لِي أُخْتٌ فَخُطِبَتْ إِلَيَّ فَكُنْتُ أَمْنَعُهَا النَّاسَ , فَأَتَى ابْنُ عَمٍّ لِي فَخَطَبَهَا فَأَنْكَحْتَهَا إِيَّاهُ , فَاصْطَحَبَا مَا شَاءَ اللَّهُ ثُمَّ طَلَّقَهَا طَلَاقًا رَجْعِيًّا ثُمَّ تَرَكَهَا حَتَّى انْقَضَتْ عِدَّتُهَا فَخَطَبَهَا مَعَ الْخُطَّابِ , فَقُلْتُ : مَنَعْتُهَا النَّاسَ وَزَوَّجْتُكَ إِيَّاهَا ثُمَّ طَلَّقْتَهَا طَلَاقًا لَهُ رَجْعَةٌ ثُمَّ تَرَكْتَهَا حَتَّى انْقَضَتْ عِدَّتُهَا فَلَمَّا خُطِبَتْ إِلَيَّ أَتَيْتِنِي تَخْطِبُهَا مَعَ الْخُطَّابِ لَا أُزَوِّجُكَ أَبَدًا فَأَنْزَلَ اللَّهُ , أَوْ قَالَ أُنْزِلَتْ : " وَإِذَا طَلَّقْتُمُ النِّسَاءَ فَبَلَغْنَ أَجَلَهُنَّ فَلَا تَعْضُلُوهُنَّ أَنْ يَنْكِحْنَ أَزْوَاجَهُنَّ " فَكَفَّرْتُ عَنْ يَمِينِي وَأَنْكَحْتُهَا إِيَّاهُ

Sayydina Mu'aqal bin Yasaar relates: I had a sister who was married to our cousin; he issued my sister with one Talaaq Rajaee. After her Iddah was complete, he wished to perform Nikah with her again. When he put the proposal forward, I prevented her from accepting his proposal. On that incident and in relation to my action this verse of the Qur'an: 'And when you have divorced women...' [2:232] was revealed, hence preventing me from prohibiting my sister to marry her former husband again.'[Qurtubi]

وَالَّذِينَ يُتَوَفَّوْنَ مِنكُمْ وَيَذَرُونَ أَزْوَاجًا يَتَرَبَّصْنَ بِأَنفُسِهِنَّ أَرْبَعَةَ أَشْهُرٍ وَعَشْرًا فَإِذَا بَلَغْنَ أَجَلَهُنَّ فَلَا جُنَاحَ عَلَيْكُمْ فِيمَا فَعَلْنَ فِي أَنفُسِهِنَّ بِالْمَعْرُوفِ وَاللَّهُ بِمَا تَعْمَلُونَ خَبِيرٌ

[2:234] Those among you who pass away and leave wives behind, their wives keep themselves waiting for four months and ten days. So, when they have reached (the end of) their waiting period, there is no sin on you in what they do for themselves in recognized manner. Allah is All-Aware of what you do.

Woman presenting herself to Nabi (Sallallaho Alaihe Wassallam) for marriage without wali (consent).

حَدَّثَنَا عَلِيُّ بْنُ عَبْدِ اللَّهِ، حَدَّثَنَا مَرْحُومٌ، قَالَ سَمِعْتُ ثَابِتًا الْبُنَانِيَّ، قَالَ كُنْتُ عِنْدَ أَنَسٍ وَعِنْدَهُ ابْنَةٌ لَهُ، قَالَ أَنَسٌ جَاءَتِ امْرَأَةٌ إِلَى رَسُولِ اللَّهِ صَلَّى اللَّهُ عَلَيْهِ وَسَلَّمَ

تَعْرِضُ عَلَيْهِ نَفْسَهَا قَالَتْ يَا رَسُولَ اللَّهِ أَلَكَ بِي حَاجَةٌ، فَقَالَتْ بِنْتُ أَنَسٍ مَا أَقَلَّ حَيَاءَهَا وَاسَوْأَتَاهُ وَاسَوْأَتَاهُ. قَالَ هِيَ خَيْرٌ مِنْكِ رَغِبَتْ فِي النَّبِيِّ صلى الله عليه وسلم فَعَرَضَتْ عَلَيْهِ نَفْسَهَا.

Sayyidina Thabit Al-Banani (RA) narrated that I was with Anas (RA) while his daughter was present with him. Anas said, "A woman came to Allah's Apostle (Sallallaho Alaihe Wassallam) and presented herself to him, saying, 'O Allah's Messenger(Sallallaho Alaihe Wassallam), have you any need for me (i.e. would you like to marry me)?' "Thereupon Anas's daughter said, "What a shameless lady she was ! Shame! Shame!" Anas said, "She was better than you; she had a liking for the Prophet (Sallallaho Alaihe Wassallam) so she presented herself for marriage to him." [Bukhari]

حَدَّثَنَا سَعِيدُ بْنُ أَبِي مَرْيَمَ، حَدَّثَنَا أَبُو غَسَّانَ، قَالَ حَدَّثَنِي أَبُو حَازِمٍ، عَنْ سَهْلٍ، أَنَّ امْرَأَةً، عَرَضَتْ نَفْسَهَا عَلَى النَّبِيِّ صلى الله عليه وسلم فَقَالَ لَهُ رَجُلٌ يَا رَسُولَ اللَّهِ زَوِّجْنِيهَا. فَقَالَ " مَا عِنْدَكَ ". قَالَ مَا عِنْدِي شَىْءٌ. قَالَ " اذْهَبْ فَالْتَمِسْ وَلَوْ خَاتَمًا مِنْ حَدِيدٍ ". فَذَهَبَ ثُمَّ رَجَعَ فَقَالَ لاَ وَاللَّهِ مَا وَجَدْتُ شَيْئًا، وَلاَ خَاتَمًا مِنْ حَدِيدٍ، وَلَكِنْ هَذَا إِزَارِي وَلَهَا نِصْفُهُ ـ قَالَ سَهْلٌ وَمَا لَهُ رِدَاءٌ. فَقَالَ النَّبِيُّ صلى الله عليه وسلم " وَمَا تَصْنَعُ بِإِزَارِكَ إِنْ لَبِسْتَهُ لَمْ يَكُنْ عَلَيْهَا مِنْهُ شَىْءٌ، وَإِنْ لَبِسَتْهُ لَمْ يَكُنْ عَلَيْكَ مِنْهُ شَىْءٌ ". فَجَلَسَ الرَّجُلُ حَتَّى إِذَا طَالَ مَجْلِسُهُ قَامَ فَرَآهُ النَّبِيُّ صلى الله عليه وسلم فَدَعَاهُ أَوْ دُعِيَ لَهُ فَقَالَ " مَاذَا مَعَكَ مِنَ الْقُرْآنِ ". فَقَالَ مَعِي سُورَةُ كَذَا وَسُورَةُ كَذَا لِسُوَرٍ يُعَدِّدُهَا. فَقَالَ النَّبِيُّ صلى الله عليه وسلم " أَمْلَكْنَاكَهَا بِمَا مَعَكَ مِنَ الْقُرْآنِ ".

Sayyidina Sahl bin Sa`d (RA) narrated that a woman presented herself to the Prophet (for marriage). A man said to him, "O Allah's Messenger (Sallallaho Alaihe Wassallam)! (If you are not in need of her) marry her to me." The Prophet (Sallallaho Alaihe Wassallam) said, "What have you got?" The man said, "I have nothing." The Prophet (Sallallaho Alaihe Wassallam) said (to him), "Go and search for something) even if it were an iron ring." The man went and returned saying, "No, I have not found anything, not even an iron ring; but this is my (Izar) waist sheet, and half of it is for her." He had no Rida' (upper garment). The Prophet (Sallallaho Alaihe Wassallam) said, "What will she do with your waist sheet? If you wear it, she will have nothing over her; and if she wears it, you will have nothing over you." So the man sat down and when he had sat a long time, he got up (to leave). When the Prophet (Sallallaho Alaihe Wassallam) saw him (leaving), he called him back, or the man was called (for him), and he said to the man, "How much of the Qur'an do you know (by heart)?" The man replied I know such Sura and such Sura (by heart)," naming the Suras The Prophet (Sallallaho Alaihe Wassallam) said, "I have married her to you for what you know of the Qur'an ." [Bukhari]

Nabi (Sallallaho Alaihe Wassallam) permitting a woman to marry without wali (consent).

وَحَدَّثَنِي عَنْ مَالِكٍ، عَنْ يَحْيَى بْنِ سَعِيدٍ، عَنْ سُلَيْمَانَ بْنِ يَسَارٍ، أَنَّ عَبْدَ اللَّهِ بْنَ عَبَّاسٍ، وَأَبَا، سَلَمَةَ بْنَ عَبْدِ الرَّحْمَنِ بْنِ عَوْفٍ اخْتَلَفَا فِي الْمَرْأَةِ تُنْفَسُ بَعْدَ وَفَاةِ زَوْجِهَا بِلَيَالٍ فَقَالَ أَبُو سَلَمَةَ إِذَا وَضَعَتْ مَا فِي بَطْنِهَا فَقَدْ حَلَّتْ . وَقَالَ ابْنُ عَبَّاسٍ آخِرَ الأَجَلَيْنِ . فَجَاءَ أَبُو هُرَيْرَةَ فَقَالَ أَنَا مَعَ ابْنِ أَخِي . يَعْنِي أَبَا سَلَمَةَ فَبَعَثُوا كُرَيْبًا مَوْلَى عَبْدِ اللَّهِ بْنِ عَبَّاسٍ إِلَى أُمِّ سَلَمَةَ زَوْجِ النَّبِيِّ صلى الله عليه وسلم يَسْأَلُهَا عَنْ ذَلِكَ فَجَاءَهُمْ فَأَخْبَرَهُمْ أَنَّهَا قَالَتْ وَلَدَتْ سُبَيْعَةُ الأَسْلَمِيَّةُ بَعْدَ وَفَاةِ زَوْجِهَا بِلَيَالٍ فَذَكَرَتْ ذَلِكَ لِرَسُولِ اللَّهِ صلى الله عليه وسلم فَقَالَ " قَدْ حَلَلْتِ فَانْكِحِي مَنْ شِئْتِ "

Yahya related to me from Malik from Yahya ibn Said from Sulayman ibn Yasar that Abdullah ibn Abbas and Abu Salama ibn Abd ar-Rahman ibn Awf differed on the question of a wornan who gave birth a few nights after the death of her husband. Abu Salama said, "When she gives birth to the child she is carrying, she is free to marry." Ibn Abbas said, "At the end of two periods." Abu Hurayra came and said, "I am with my nephew", meaning Abu Salama. They sent Kurayb, a mawla of Abdullah ibn Abbas to Umm Salama, the wife of the Prophet, may Allah bless him and grant him peace, to ask her about it. He came back and told them that she had said that Subaya al-Aslamiya had given birth a few nights after the death of her husband, and she had brought the matter to the Messenger of Allah, may Allah bless him and grant him peace, and he had said, "You are free to marry, so marry whomever you wish." [Muwatta]

Nabi (Sallallaho Alaihe Wassallam) marrying Umm Salamah (RA) without wali (consent).

من طريق عمر بن أبي سلمة عن أم سلمة قالت: دخل عليّ رسول الله صلى الله عليه وسلم بعد وفاة أبي سلمة، فخطبني إلى نفسي فقلت: يا رسول الله؛ إنه ليس أحد من أوليائي شاهداً. فقال: (إنه ليس منهم شاهد ولا غائب يكره ذلك). قالت: قم يا عمر. فزوج النبي صلى الله عليه وسلم، فتزوجها

Sayyidah Umme Salama related, when her Iddah was completed following the death of her husband, the Prophet sent her a proposal for marriage. She responded to the Prophet: 'my guardian is not present here.' The Prophet responded: 'whether your guardians are present or not, they will not disapprove of this Nikah.' Then Umme Salama said to her young (immature) son: 'O Umar come accompany me at my Nikah. [Tahawi]

Nabi (Sallallaho Alaihe Wassallam) explicitly stating the rights of previously married woman to herself.

وَحَدَّثَنَا قُتَيْبَةُ بْنُ سَعِيدٍ، حَدَّثَنَا سُفْيَانُ، عَنْ زِيَادِ بْنِ سَعْدٍ، عَنْ عَبْدِ اللَّهِ بْنِ الْفَضْلِ، سَمِعَ نَافِعَ بْنَ جُبَيْرٍ، يُخْبِرُ عَنِ ابْنِ عَبَّاسٍ، أَنَّ النَّبِيَّ صلى الله عليه وسلم قَالَ " الثَّيِّبُ أَحَقُّ بِنَفْسِهَا مِنْ وَلِيِّهَا وَالْبِكْرُ تُسْتَأْمَرُ وَإِذْنُهَا سُكُوتُهَا "

Sayyidina Ibn Abbas (RA) reported Allah's Messenger (Sallallaho Alaihe Wassallam) as saying: A woman who has been previously married (Thayyib) has more right to her person than her guardian. And a virgin should also be consulted, and her silence implies her consent. [Muslim]

Nabi (Sallallaho Alaihe Wassallam) explicitly ordering to seek consent from a woman.

حَدَّثَنِي عُبَيْدُ اللَّهِ بْنُ عُمَرَ بْنِ مَيْسَرَةَ الْقَوَارِيرِيُّ، حَدَّثَنَا خَالِدُ بْنُ الْحَارِثِ، حَدَّثَنَا هِشَامٌ، عَنْ يَحْيَى بْنِ أَبِي كَثِيرٍ، حَدَّثَنَا أَبُو سَلَمَةَ، حَدَّثَنَا أَبُو هُرَيْرَةَ، أَنَّ رَسُولَ اللَّهِ صلى الله عليه وسلم قَالَ " لاَ تُنْكَحُ الأَيِّمُ حَتَّى تُسْتَأْمَرَ وَلاَ تُنْكَحُ الْبِكْرُ حَتَّى تُسْتَأْذَنَ " . قَالُوا يَا رَسُولَ اللَّهِ وَكَيْفَ إِذْنُهَا قَالَ " أَنْ تَسْكُتَ

Sayyidina Abu Huraira (RA) reported Allah's Messenger (Sallallaho Alaihe Wassallam) as having said: A woman without a husband (or divorced or a widow) must not be married until she is consulted, and a virgin must not be married until her permission is sought. They asked the Prophet of Allah (Sallallaho Alaihe Wassallam): How her (virgin's) consent can be solicited? He (the Holy Prophet) said: That she keeps silence. [Bukhari]

Sayyida Aisha (RA) marrying a girl without the permission of her Wali!

وَحَدَّثَنِي عَنْ مَالِكٍ، عَنْ عَبْدِ الرَّحْمَنِ بْنِ الْقَاسِمِ، عَنْ أَبِيهِ، أَنَّ عَائِشَةَ زَوْجَ النَّبِيِّ صَلَّى اللَّهُ عَلَيْهِ وَسَلَّمَ " زَوَّجَتْ حَفْصَةَ بِنْتَ عَبْدِ الرَّحْمَنِ الْمُنْذِرَ بْنَ الزُّبَيْرِ، وَعَبْدُ الرَّحْمَنِ غَائِبٌ بِالشَّامِ، فَلَمَّا قَدِمَ عَبْدُ الرَّحْمَنِ، قَالَ: " وَمِثْلِي يُصْنَعُ هَذَا بِهِ، وَمِثْلِي يُفْتَاتُ عَلَيْهِ؟ فَكَلَّمَتْ عَائِشَةُ الْمُنْذِرَ بْنَ الزُّبَيْرِ، فَقَالَ الْمُنْذِرُ: فَإِنَّ ذَلِكَ بِيَدِ عَبْدِ الرَّحْمَنِ، فَقَالَ عَبْدُ الرَّحْمَنِ: مَا كُنْتُ لأَرُدَّ أَمْرًا قَضَيْتِهِ، فَقَرَّتْ حَفْصَةُ عِنْدَ الْمُنْذِرِ، وَلَمْ يَكُنْ ذَلِكَ طَلاَقًا "

It was reported in Al Muwatta' on the authority of `Abdur-Rahman ibn Al Qasim from his father from `A'ishah (RA) that she gave Hafsah bint `Abdur-Rahman in marriage to Al Mundhir ibn Az-Zubayr while `Abdur-Rahman was away in Syria. When `Abdur-Rahman arrived, he said: "Shall someone like me have this done to him? Am I the kind of man to have something done to him without his consent?" `A'ishah (may Allah be pleased with her) spoke to Al Mundhir ibn Az-Zubayr, and Al Mundhir said: " It is in the hands of `Abdur-Rahman ." `Abdur-Rahman said: "I will not oppose something that you have already completed." Hafsah stayed with Al Mundhir, and there was no divorce. [Muwatta]

Counter evidence?

The narrations presented which quote the marriage of a woman without wali (consent) to be invalid are considered weak by many Masters of Hadeeth; although some do regard them as authentic.

The actions of Sayyida Aisha (RA) recorded in Muwatta after the passing away of Nabi (Sallallaho Alaihe Wassallam) in giving away the daughter of Sayyidina Abdur-Rahman (RA) without his consent clearly demonstrate her understanding of the matter.

The marriage of the daughter Sayyidina Abdur-Rahman (RA) was neither invalidated nor her Nikah performed (again).

Does the Hanafi School encourage marriage without the guardian's (wali) approval?

Shaykh (Mufti) Muhammad ibn Adam (HA)

In the name of Allah, Most Compassionate, Most Merciful,

The short and simple answer to your question is that: No, the Hanafi School does not, in any way, promote or encourage a marriage without the approval of one's parents or a legal guardian (wali).

To elaborate: It is a common misconception that the Hanafi School unreservedly allows a marriage without the consent of the woman's parents or her guardian (wali). However, the matter is not as simple as that, and one must understand the Hanafi position properly before coming to any sort of conclusion.

In contrast to the position of most other scholars including the three Sunni Schools of Islamic law, the Hanafi School indeed has some leeway in regards to the necessity of obtaining the consent of the woman's guardian. The relied upon position within the School is that the marriage of a free, sane and adult woman without the approval of her guardian (wali) is valid if the person she is marrying is a "legal" and suitable match (kuf') to her. Conversely, if the person she is marrying is not a legal match to her, then her marriage is considered invalid. (Radd al-Muhtar ala 'l-Durr al-Mukhtar 3/56-57 & I'la al-Sunan 11/69. For more details and the relevant evidences, please refer to the answer previously posted on this website titled: "Divorced woman marrying without her guardian's approval").

However, this does not mean that such a marriage is encouraged or permitted without any blame. Disobeying one's parents is one of the most serious of sins in Islam, and as such, no School would, and can, allow going against the wishes of one's parents outright. Many Hanafi jurists (fuqaha) have pointed out that it is generally blameworthy and going against the Sunnah to marry without the consent of the Wali regardless of whether the spouse is a legal match or otherwise due to the many Hadiths of the Messenger of Allah (Allah bless him & give him peace) emphasising the importance of having the approval of one's guardian such as: "Any woman who marries without the permission of her guardian, her marriage is invalid, invalid, invalid" (related by Ibn Hibban, Tirmidhi and others, and Tirmidhi considered it a sound/hasan Hadith) and: "There is no marriage without the [permission of a] guardian" (related by Hakim and Abu Dawud). (See: Imdad al-Muftin P: 527)

As such, this Hanafi position is merely a concession (rukhsa) which may be resorted to in situations of need, and a blessing for those sisters who fall victim to their parent's mistreatment and abuse. In cases where parents force their daughters to marry against their wishes based purely on caste, wealth and other similar preferences, and not Islam, and they give importance to their personal gains over and above the interests of their daughters; this position of the Hanafi School can be an important haven. However, the Hanafi School, in no way, gives a green light for sisters to marry themselves without parental approval in all situations, and as such, this position must not be taken as a standard norm upon which marriage contracts are based.

Thus, a woman must first try and convince her parents or Wali to allow her to marry according to her wishes. She may use the intermediary of someone who may be able to influence her parents. Despite trying, if her parents are still being difficult, and her wish is to marry someone based on religious piety, she should present her case to a knowledge, wise and god-fearing scholar who may be able to advise whether she may marry without her guardian's approval or not.

And Allah knows best

[Mufti]Muhammad ibn Adam
Darul Iftaa, Leicester , UK

Nikah & Walima Dilemma: Planning Trips & Tricks!

Allah's Messenger (Sallallaho Alaihe Wassallam) said, "When a man marries he has fulfilled half of the 'deen'; so let him fear Allah regarding the remaining half." [Tirmidhi].

Mubarak (congratulations), so you have found someone to be your comfort in this world and the next and may Allah (SWT) make all your dreams come true, fill your life with bliss and happiness (Ameen).

We have an exclusive section on the Fiqh issues relating to relationships, marriage, sexuality, children so this article will briefly look at the actual planning and execution of one of the biggest days of your life.

We often find people engaged in Culture vs. Islam discussions and the couple (to be wed) often at odds with their family and parents over the planning and execution of events. Aspects of culture which are not exclusively forbidden in Islam are permissible so before arguing with the "elders" of your family know what is permitted and what isn't!

Get your intention right!

The blessings and assistance of Allah (SWT) are only with following the noble Sunnah of Sayyidina Rasul-ullah (Sallallaho Alaihe Wassallam), understand it and continue to remind yourself and the family members that every action has repercussions. Good actions will bring good repercussions and bad actions will bring calamity.

[3:31] Say (O Prophet): If you really love Allah, then follow me, and Allah shall love you and forgive you your sins. Allah is Most-Forgiving, Very-Merciful.

Don't do the action if you are not prepared to live with the consequences as we say in America!

Don't do the crime, if you can't do the time!

Family Meeting (Mushwara):

[42:38] and those who have responded to their Lord (in submission to Him), and have established Salah, and whose affairs are (settled) with mutual consultation between them, and who spend out of what We have given to them.

Not only its polite and courteous to ask your elders and family members for advice, Shura is a command of Allah (SWT) so consult friends and family members with the intention of fulfilling a command of Allah (SWT) and it will pay dividends in your later life as they will remember that you asked for their advice.

Budget & Expenses:

In our experience this is the single most misunderstood aspect of wedding plans. On one extreme Muslims are under the impression that they are supposed to be as cheap as possible while on the other hand there are those who want to outdo others in spending. The command of Allah (SWT) is to be moderate (according to your means).

[17:29] And do not keep your hand tied to your neck, nor extend it to the full extent, lest you should be sitting reproached, empty-handed.

It is true that you are supposed to have a simple wedding but the term "simple" is subjective and varies according to personal circumstances, "simple" for a billionaire has different connotations compared to someone who is hand to mouth and noting the

15

extravagance of today the billionaire will be rewarded for conducting his (or her) wedding according to the budget of someone who is hand to mouth but if he (or she) conducts a "simple" ceremony (according to their standard) and doesn't compromise any commands or tenants of Qur'aan & Sunnah then it will be permissible.

Avoiding Extravagance & Debt!

You should marry within your means and avoid the current trend of showing off and extravagance because extravagance is Haram. Renew your intention and know that if you want to follow the path of Shaytaan then be prepared for the consequences.

> [17:26] Give the relative his right, and the needy and the wayfarer. And do not squander recklessly. [17:27] Surely, squanderers are brothers of satans, and the Satan is very ungrateful to his Lord.

It goes without saying that Debt should be avoided as much as possible. However, many families sometimes have no choice and if you need to borrow money for legitimate and Shariah compliant needs then keep two principles in mind:

Avoid Interest: You cannot start your new life by declaring a war upon Allah (SWT) and Sayyidina Rasul-ullah (Sallallaho Alaihe Wassallam)! The consequences will be disastrous as nothing good will come out of an interest bearing loan, at all!

> [2:278] O you who believe, fear Allah and give up what still remains of riba, if you are believers. [2:279] But if you do not (give it up), then listen to the declaration of war from Allah and His Messenger. However, If you repent, yours is your principal. Neither wrong, nor be wronged.

Loan Contract: There are countless families who took loans for weddings and then get embroiled into lifelong feuds simply because they didn't follow the Qur'aanic commandments of

16

loan agreement. Have your transactions written down and witnessed and avoid hassles for later!

[2:282] O you who believe, when you transact a debt payable at a specified time, put it in writing, and let a scribe write it between you with fairness. A scribe should not refuse to write as Allah has educated him. He, therefore, should write. The one who owes something should get it written, but he must fear Allah, his Lord, and he should not omit anything from it. If the one who owes is feeble-minded or weak or cannot dictate himself, then his guardian should dictate with fairness. Have two witnesses from among your men, and if two men are not there, then one man and two women from those witnesses whom you like, so that if one of the two women errs, the other woman may remind her. The witnesses should not refuse when summoned. And do not be weary of writing it down, along with its due date, no matter whether the debt is small or large. That is more equitable in Allah's sight, and more supportive as evidence, and more likely to make you free of doubt. However, if it is a spot transaction you are effecting between yourselves, there is no sin on you, should you not write it. Have witnesses when you transact a sale. Neither a scribe should be made to suffer, nor a witness. If you do (something harmful to them), it is certainly a sin on your part, and fear Allah. Allah educates you, and Allah is All-Knowing in respect of everything.

You cannot start your new life by declaring a war upon Allah (SWT) and Sayyidina Rasul-ullah (Sallallaho Alaihe Wassallam)! The consequences will be disastrous as nothing good will come out of an interest bearing loan, at all!

The issue of Jahaiz (Dowry) amongst Asians:

The primary responsibility of taking care and looking after a woman belongs to the man. In fact, Allah (SWT) has made men superior because they financially spend on women.

[4:34] Men are caretakers of women, since Allah has made some of them excel the others, and because of the wealth they have spent.

It is shameful for a man or his family to go begging to the family of a Muslim woman or to insinuate (or hint) indirectly or covertly demand an amount of money or mode of transportation (car, motorbike) etc. In fact, the man and his family should make it clear in explicit terms that they don't need anything because in the Asian culture it is often assumed that certain things are needed and provided without request. **Scholars of Islam explicitly advise Muslim men to buck the trend and break the shackles of the curse of Jahaiz (dowry).**

One of the most abused Ahadeeth of Sayyidina Rasul-ullah (Sallallaho Alaihe Wassallam) amonst the Asians is as follows:

> On the occasion of the Nikah of Sayyidah Fatima (RA) the Prophet Muhammad (Sallallaho Alaihe Wassallam) gave her as gifts: a blanket filled with date palm leaves, a leather pillow and a clay water pot. [Nisai]

The Prophet Muhammad (Sallallaho Alaihe Wassallam) was the guardian of both Sayyidina Ali (RA) and Sayyidah Fatima (RA) . Therefore The Prophet Muhammad (Sallallaho Alaihe Wassallam) on behalf of Sayyidina Ali made this arrangement so that the obligation of Sayyidina Ali (RA) would be fulfilled. There is no proof from the Ahadith that the Prophet did this for any of his other daughters Nikah. There was no tradition of Jahaiz during the time of Prophet Muhammad , nor during the time of the Sahaaba.(Mariful Hadith vol 7, p30)

The issue of Meh'r (Dowry) amongst Arabs:

The Arabs have the exact opposite problem where they have taken a command of Allah (SWT) and exaggerated it to such proportions that it's become next to impossible in many Arab countries to find a wife. Meh'r (dowry) is a command of Allah (SWT) and right of the women:

> [4:4] Give women their dower in good cheer. Then, if they forego some of it, of their own will, you may have it as pleasant and joyful.

There are no examples from the noble Sunnah of Sayyidina Rasul-ullah (Sallallaho Alaihe Wassallam) or companions where women set such exorbitant amounts which created marriage epidemics (as evident in Middle-East today). The noble example of our Nabi (Sallallaho Alaihe Wassallam) for us to follow is as follow:

Abu Salama Ibn 'Abd al-Rahman (RA) reported: I asked 'A'isha (RA) the wife of Allah's Messenger (may peace be upon him): What is the amount of dower of Allah's Messenger (may peace be upon him)? She said: It was twelve 'uqiyas and one nash. She said: Do you know what is al-nash? I said: No. She said: It is half of uqiya, and it amounts to five hundred dirhams, and that was the dower given by Allah's Messenger (may peace be upon him) to his wives. [Muslim]

Not only the prophet didn't pay exorbitant amounts of money to be married but he also discouraged this practise and advised that the best of the women are the ones who are light (in their Meh'r):

Sayyidina 'Uqbah ibn 'Aamir (RA) narrates the Prophet(Sallallaho Alaihe Wassallam) said: "The best dowry is that which is easy." [Hakim]

The issue of Haq Meh'r (Dowry) amongst Asians:

In the prevalent Asian culture two misconceptions exist with regards to Meh'r:

It is thought that Me'h is only due upon divorce.

Since it is only thought to be due upon divorce exorbitant amounts are set (and competed within families) and publicised as a status symbol.

Both of these absurdities have nothing to do with Islam! The agreed amount becomes an obligation upon the husband and needs to be paid as per the agreed terms and conditions **discussed in detail here**.

Actual Financial Planning:

Don't start planning without an actual cap or estimation of your spending because things will quickly get out of hand and note that you will go through several iterations of a budget planner depending on your circumstances. The actual expenses, arrangements and the breakdown will vary from place to place and some of these given below may be paid for by the Bride (or the Groom's) family, nevertheless here is a starting point for planning. Don't go into a wedding without having an idea of the expenses!

Wedding Invitation Printing	**$250.00**
Walima Inviation Printing	$250.00
Wedding Clothes (couple and family)	$1,000.00
Wedding Hall	$300.00
Walima Hall	$300.00
Wedding (Food + Catering) @ $25/head	$5,000.00
Walima (Food + Catering) @ $25/head	$5,000.00
Wedding Decorations	$500.00
Walima Decorations	$500.00
Guest (Housing) Expenses	$500.00
Total	$13,600.00

Guest Invitation List:

Your budget will actually dictate the guests whom you can invite and cater for within your means. Don't take creating a guest list lightly as soon you will discover that things will go out of hand and you will either forget someone or invite someone with a family while ignore someone (equally importantly) without their family. A sample is presented below

Groom's Father's older brother (Family)	**7**
Bride's Father's older brother (Family)	9
Groom's Father's second older brother (Family)	5
Bride's Father's second older brother (Family)	3
Groom's Father's older Sister (Family)	6
Bride's Father's older Sister (Family)	4
Groom's Father's second older Sister (Family)	5
Bride's Father's second older Sister (Family)	4
Groom's Father's best friend (Family)	5
Bride's Father's best friend (Family)	4
Total	52

Non-Muslim Customs:

Following the customs of Non-Muslims is Haram and it will not only destroy the blessings in your wedding but will also drown you in debt! It is harmful for your worldly life and detrimental for your hereafter. Two of the most common customs amonst Asians which have nothing to do with Islam are:

Mayon: This is an Asian custom conducted a few days before the actual wedding which has absolutely nothing to with Islam and directly imported from Hindu'ism. The uncontrolled intermingling of genders, singing, dancing and merrymaking make it explicitly Haram.

Mehndi: This is an Asian custom conducted a few days before the actual wedding which has absolutely nothing to with Islam and directly imported from Hindu'ism. To apply Mehndi (Henna) is Sunnah for the women but to turn a Sunnah into an event has no basis in Islam. The uncontrolled intermingling of genders, singing, dancing and merrymaking make it explicitly Haram.

Muslims of other parts of the world may have their own customs which need to be discussed with Scholars.

Conducting Nikah at the Masjid:

Shaykh (Mufti) Ibraheem Desai writes, "It is Sunnah for the marriage to be pronounced and performed in the Masjid". The decision to conduct the Nikah at the Masjid will not only bring Barakah in your marriage but will also cut down (and Insha'Allah) prohibit violations of Islamic Shariah.

Aisha (RA) narrated that Rasul-ullah (Sallaho Alaihe Wassallam) said, "Publicise these marriages, conduct them in mosques, and beat the duff (tambourines) to announce them". [Tirmidhi]

Wedding/Walima Dress, Photography & Video:

It is praiseworthy for the potential spouses to dress nicely and to appear pleasing for each other. However some things must be kept in mind:

It is Haram to beautify the girl and then place her on a stage for everyone to feast their eyes on her beauty.

Most people will dress for the occasion so it's Haram to have a mixed gathering where unhindered and unfettered access and intermingling to opposite sex is available. This is a gateway to Fitnah so ensure that your wedding is segregated.

Photographer or the one making the move is not exempt from the laws of Islamic Shariah and cannot wander in and out of both sections unhindered and unchecked. A Sister recently sent a question to our site stating that she is soon to be married and then her husband needs to apply for US immigration and they have been legally advised that the wedding photographs and movie may need to be submitted (or asked later) during the immigration process. This is true and in such cases extreme care needs to be taken that photographs are not taken with Na-Mehrams and not shared with them (afterwards). During our discussions with families, we often come across this question and it can be handled with delicacy and tact and the photographs and the movie needs to handled with due care.

Many amongst the Asians require the Groom to wear a suit (and tie) on their Nikah and although this cannot be regarded as impermissible but care should be taken that it isn't a pure silk suit or a pure silk tie (extremely common). It is permissible for men to wear artificial silk but not desirable.

It is impermissible to play Music in Islamic Shariah on wedding day or otherwise, however this can be easily substituted with Nasheeds without Music. Many artists like Junaid Jamshaid and others have Nasheeds for multiples occasions without Music.

It is a custom amongst Asians to form a Bar'aat which is a collective of family and friends who travel together for Nikah, there is anything inherently wrong with it provided that intermingling and free mixing of sexes doesn't occur.

Wedding/Walima on the same day:

We have come across examples of families conducting the Nikah and Walima on the same day. Although it is superior to perform Walima after the couple have consummated the marriage or had had some privacy, the Sunnah of Walima will be rendered discharged if conducted on the same day without the couple having had the chance of privacy.

Wedding/Walima Food (Serving & Arrangemenst):

The rules of prohibition with regards to Intermingling and free mixing still apply during the serving and partaking of food. We have witnessed many weddings where the organizers have gone through the trouble of organizing a segregated wedding but at the reception the rules of segregation either don't exist or are relaxed (i.e.) people wandering in and out of both sections on the pretense of serving or filling dishes.

However, in our experience we have encountered (unfortunately) strong resistance from families on this issue so the next best compromise is to create a seating plan and create really nice and pleasing tables and chairs. Ensure that some of the guests (close family and friends) and given priority seating! Ensure that all guests are seen to and welcomed in and out of the Hall (Masjid).

Honeymoon planning?

There is no such concept in Honeymoon in Islamic Fiqh but for the newlywed couple to go out and spend time together in isolation in order to come to know each other is permissible.

Recommended Reading:

We strongly encourage and recommend everyone to read this beneficial pamphlet on the subject by Shaykh (Maulana) Saleem Dhorat (HA).

Khul & Tafweedh: Wife initiated Separation

In the situation where a woman can no longer remain in the marriage of her husband and all attempts to save the marriage have failed, then the ideal solution would be for her to obtain a divorce from the husband.

About Seperation Initiated by the Wife (khul' or Khula)

By Shaykh (Mufti) Muhammad Ibn Adam (HA)

Question: There is a Muslim sister who was married to a brother. At the time, they were both not praying, fasting or anything. She was not wearing hijab either. Then she changed. She started to wear the hijaab, pray, fast, and has now adopted the niqaab and is seeking knowledge as well as the principal advisor of an Islamic school.

Her husband is still not praying nor does he intend to as he has told her. She and he have had many arguments and he still will not pray. The mother was commanded by the husband on many occasions to take of the niqaab when she is with him in public and at one moment in time, he ripped it from her face and drug her inside, so that she could not leave the house to do her principal duties at the Islamic school.

This has been going on for quite a few years. Now the sister wants a divorce. He does not, so then she decided to seek khula. But I wanted to know, due to the fact that she has asked me, how is the khula procedure in the Hanafi school as well as if the following make any difference.

He has not paid her the mahr that he promised her on the marriage day.

There are four children involved

Does an imam have to be involved to initiate the khula from one side if the husband says that he does not want to?

Must the wife pay the husband and how is this affected if he has not given her the mahr? How would she give him half the value or the value of the mahr that he gave her when he has not given her the mahr as of yet?

Is she to wait 1 cycle or two in the Hanafi School upon completing the khula?

She has explained that every time that she sees him she feels sick and she has prayed istikhaara numerous times and has no doubt in her heart that she does not want to be married to him any longer.

There has been and has recently been physical violence against her by the husband as well as in front of the children.

Answer: In the Name of Allah, Most Compassionate, Most Merciful,

In the situation where a woman can no longer remain in the marriage of her husband and all attempts to save the marriage have failed, then the ideal solution would be for her to obtain a divorce from the husband. The husband, seeing that the marriage is futile and there is no hope of reconcilement, should also issue one divorce according to the prescribed method in Shariah.

However, in the case where the husband refuses to issue a divorce, the wife may persuade the husband to enter into an agreement of Khul' (a release for payment from the wife). The wife may also opt to forgive the husband from paying her dowry (mahr).

Khul' is an Arabic term that literally means 'to take out' and 'remove'. The Arabs say: "Khala'tu al-libas" (I took off my cloths). Similarly, Allah Almighty said to Sayyiduna Musa (Peace be upon him) when he went to receive the sacred law:

"Verily I am your lord! Therefore, take off (fakhla') your shoes." (Surah Ta Ha, 12)

The lexical definition of Khul' as explained by the famous Hanafi Mujtahid, Ibn Humam is as follows:

"To remove the union of marriage in exchange of a financial settlement with the words of Khul." (Ibn Humam, Fath al-Qadir, 3/1999)

Similar to other agreements and transactions, an agreement on Khul' will also come into effect by acceptance and offer. (al-Kasani, Bada'i al- Sana'i, 3/145 & Radd al-Muhtar, 2/606)

The couple can normally agree upon any financial arrangement they desire. However, the Fuqaha state that, if the husband was at fault and it was his wrongdoings that resulted in the failure of their marriage, then it is impermissible for him to demand a financial payment in return for a divorce. He should divorce the wife without demanding anything in return.

Allah Most High says:

"But if you decide to take one wife in place of another, even if you had given the latter a whole treasure for dower, take not the least bit of it back. Would you take it by slander and a manifest wrong? And how could you take it when you have gone into each other, and We have taken from you a solemn covenant?" (Surah al-Nisa, 20-21)

Due to the above verse of the Qur'an, the Fuqaha have declared the taking of anything in return as a major sin if the husband was at fault.

However, if the husband was not at fault, but the wife for some reason or another wishes to end the marriage, then it is permissible for the husband to demand and receive some financial payment. It would be superior for him not to take more than the actual stipulated dowry. However, it would be permissible for them to agree on any amount. (See: Bada'i al-Sana'i, 3/150 & Bahr al-Ra'iq, 4/83)

Allah Most High says:

"It is unlawful for you (men), to take back (dowry, etc...) from your wives, except when both parties fear that they would be unable to keep the limits ordained by Allah. If you (judges) do indeed fear that they would be unable to keep the limits ordained by Allah, there is no blame on either of them if she gives something for her freedom." (Surah al-Baqarah, 229)

According to the Majority of Jurists (jumhur), a Khula' agreement can be carried out without having to go to an Islamic court. Merely, the consent of both parties is sufficient. (See: al-Sarakhsi, al-Mabsut, 6/173)

A Khul' is considered an irrevocable divorce and a finalized cancellation of marriage (ba'in), differing from a threefold divorce by the fact that they may remarry in such a case without her marrying another husband first.

If they did remarry, the husband will only remain the owner of two more divorces. Meaning, if he further issued two more divorces, it will total to three, thus he will not be able to take her back until she marries another man. (See: al-Mabsut, 6/173)

The waiting period (idda) for the woman will be similar to that of a woman who was given an irrevocable divorce (ba'in) which is three menstrual cycles. The husband can not take her back within or after the waiting period without her consent (by contracting a new agreement of marriage).

Finally, it should also be remembered that a Khul' agreement can only be carried out with the consent of the husband. The wife does not have the jurisdiction to enforce Khul' without the consent of her husband. This is an agreed upon ruling in all of the four Sunni schools of Islamic law.

The great Hanafi jurist, Imam al-Sarakhsi says:

"An agreement of Khul' is permissible with or without the presence of a judge, as it is a contract that is based on mutual agreement." (al-Mabsut, 6/173)

The same has also been mentioned in Radd al-Muhtar, al-Fatawa al-Hindiyya and other major works.

With the above discussion, I sincerely hope all your queries with regards to Khul' have been answered.

And Allah Knows Best

[Mufti] Muhammad ibn Adam

Darul Iftaa

Leicester , UK

Financial Support when Seperation Initiated by the Wife (khul' or Khula)

Shaykh (Mufti) Zubair Dudha (HA)

Question: Is a Muslim woman entitled financial support and upkeep from her (former) husband when she has initiated separation and applied for Khul? And if so for how long?

Answer: In the Name of Allah, Most Compassionate, Most Merciful,

The Muslim woman is entitled to maintenance unless she explicitly forgoes her rights as part of the agreement. This maintenance will need to be provided until her Iddah period expires.

And Allah Knows Best

[Mufti] Zubair Dudha

Islamic Tarbiyah Academy (ITA)

45 Boothroyd Lane, West Town,
Dewsbury, WF13 2RB, United Kingdom
Tel-Fax: +44(1924) 450422

Delegating the Right of Divorce to the Wife (Tafwidh)

By Shaykh (Mufti) Muhammad Ibn Adam (HA)

Question: Is it valid for a woman to put as a stipulation in a written Islamic contract that she will have the open right to divorce, as opposed to her naming the specific conditions under which this right will be carried out?

Also the woman's father is representing the bride at the nikah ceremony, she will not actually be present during the nikah; how will this contract be signed and presented in her absence?

Answer: In the Name of Allah, Most Compassionate, Most Merciful,

According to Shariah, the right to divorce belongs primarily to the husband and not the wife. There are many reasons and wisdoms behind this ruling, which have been explained in detail in an earlier post.

However, although the power to issue a divorce belongs in principle to the husband, he may delegate this power to his wife or a third party, with or without stipulating conditions. Once this power is delegated, it can not be revoked or withdrawn. This is known in the Fiqh terminology as "Tafwid".

This is based upon the incident where the Messenger of Allah (Allah bless him & give him peace) gave his wives the option to remain in his marriage or be divorced. Allah Most High said to the Messenger of Allah (Allah bless him & give him peace):

"O Prophet! Say to your wives: "If it be that you desire the life of this world, and its glitter, then come! I will provide for your enjoyment and set you free in a handsome manner. But if you seek Allah and His Messenger, and the Home of the Hereafter, verily Allah has prepared for the well-doers amongst you a great reward." (Surah al-Ahzab, 28)

The Messenger of Allah (Allah bless him & give him peace) deserted his wives for a period of around one month, after which the above verse was revealed.

Sayyida A'isha (Allah be pleased with her) narrates: "When the Messenger of Allah (Allah bless him & give him peace) was commanded to give an option (of divorce) to his wives, he started with me saying: "I am going to mention to you a matter in which you should not (decide) hastily until you have consulted your parents." She (A'isha) said that he already knew that my parents would never instruct me to seek separation from him. She said: "Then he said: Allah, the Exalted and Glorious, said: "O Prophet, say to your wives: If it be that you desire the life of this World, and its glitter, then come! I will provide for your enjoyment and set you free in a handsome manner. But if you seek Allah and His Messenger, and the Home of the Hereafter, verily Allah has prepared for the well-doers amongst you a great reward." Sayyida A'isha (Allah be pleased with her) says that I said to the Messenger of Allah (Allah bless him & give him peace): "About this should I consult my parents, for I desire Allah and His Messenger and the abode of the Hereafter?" She (A'isha) said: "Then all the wives of the Messenger of Allah (Allah bless him & give him peace) did as I had done." (Sahih Muslim, no. 1475)

Sayyida A'isha (Allah be pleased with her) also narrates that the Messenger of Allah (Allah bless him & give him peace) gave us the option (m: to remain with him or to be divorced), so we chose (and preferred) Allah and His Messenger. Giving us that option was not regarded as a divorce." (Sahih al-Bukhari, no. 4962)

Imam al-Sarakhsi (Allah have mercy on him) states:

"If a man delegates the right to divorce to his wife, then this is similar to giving an option (khiyar) in trade, except that this is completely valid and logical, for the husband is the owner of issuing the divorce, thus he is in a position of delegating something that he owns. Hence, it will be binding, in that the husband will not have the right to revoke this delegation." (al-Mabsut, 7/221)

The Companions (Sahaba, Allah be pleased with them all) also unanimously agreed upon the validity of delegating the right to divorce to the wife. (See: al-Mawsili, al-Ikhtiyar li ta'lil al-Mukhtar, 2/166 & Zaylai'i, Nab al-Raya, 3/229)

Rules concerning the delegation of the right to divorce (tafwid)

There are certain rules and regulations with regards to this delegation that need to be understood properly:

When the husband delegates the right to divorce to the wife, she will only have this right in the session (majlis) that she is in. If she did not exercise her right, then this right will go in vain. However, if the husband delegates this right for a specific period (e.g. 5 years) or permanently, then she will have this right accordingly. (Radd al-Muhtar & al-Ikhtiyar)

The wife will only have a right to divorce herself according to what was delegated to her. If the husband delegated to her the right to divorce herself once (and not two or three times), or he delegated the right to divorce herself irrevocably, then she will have this right accordingly. She will only be allowed to utilize this right in a manner it was delegated to her. (Radd al-Muhtar)

If the husband gave his wife the right to divorce herself a specific number of divorces, then she will not have a right to divorce herself more than the number of divorces that were delegated to her.

Once the husband delegates this right to his wife, he can not overturn or revoke it. (Durr al-Mukhtar)

If the right to divorce was delegated for a specific period of time and the wife did not utilize this right in that period, then upon the termination of this period, the right will also no longer remain. (al-Ikhtiyar)

By delegating the right to divorce, the husband still has a right to divorce his wife. Delegation of this right does not imply that the husband no longer has a right to issue a divorce. (al-Ikhtiyar)

If the wife rejects accepting this right of divorcing herself, then if the delegation was permanent, her rejection will be of no consequence, in that she will still have this right permanently despite rejecting the offer. However, if this delegation was not permanent, then by rejection, the right to divorce will terminate. (al-Ikhtiyar)

Different stages of delegation

There are different stages and times when the man delegates the right to divorce to the woman. In summary, there are three situations here:

If the delegation (tafwid) took place after the spouses had entered into wedlock, then this, without doubt, can be done. However, the husband here will be free to accept this, as he is already in the marriage.

The second situation is when this delegation (tafwid) takes place at the time of contracting the marriage.

This is also permissible and valid, provided one condition is met, which is that the offer of marriage is initiated by the woman coupled with the demand for Tafwid, and the man accepts this. If the opposite takes place, it will be void.

Imam al-Haskafi (Allah have mercy on him) states:

"If the man married her on condition that she will have the right to divorce herself, then this will be valid."

Allama Ibn Abidin (Allah have mercy no him) commentates on this by saying:

34

"(Imam al-Haskafi's statement "this will be valid"), this is subject to the condition that the woman initiates the contract of marriage with her offer by saying: "I marry myself to you on the condition that I will have the right to divorce myself whenever I wish" and the husband says: "I accept this". However, if the husband initiated the contract of marriage, she will not have a right to divorce herself, as mentioned in al-Bahr." (Radd al-Muhtar ala al-Durr, 3/329)

Thus, if the woman (or her representative) initiated the marriage contract by the offer (ijab) and asked for the right to divorce, then she will be entitled to this right, and whenever she divorces herself, it will be valid.

The third stage of Tafwid is when it takes place before the actual contract of marriage. In other words, the woman demands the right to divorce herself if they are to get married.

This is also permissible and valid, but also subject to one condition, that the husband attributes the Tafwid to the marriage. Meaning he says: "If I marry you, then you have the right to issue one irrevocable divorce upon yourself." However, if the man did not attribute this to the marriage, it will be void.

It is stated in Durr al-Mukhtar:

"The condition of its validity is having ownership (m: by actual marriage) or referring it to the marriage...such as he says: "If I marry you, then you are divorced (m: or you have the right to divorce yourself)." (See: Radd al-Muhtar ala al-Durr al-Mukhtar, 3/344 & al-Ikhtiyar, 2/ 170)

As far as your second question is concerned, the woman can appoint her father as her representative (wakil) to contract the marriage on her behalf. It is not necessary for the woman to be present in the session of the marriage contract. Her representative will have the same authority as she herself has.

And Allah Knows Best

[Mufti] Muhammad ibn Adam

Darul Iftaa Leicester , UK

The Fiqh of Adopting a Child

Adopting someone else's child, bringing it up, seeing to its education and training and being kind and good towards him/her is very virtuous and a commendable act. If the child is an orphan and has no support, then the reward is much more.

The Fiqh of Adopting a Child

By Shaykh (Mufti) Muhammad Ibn Adam (HA)

Question: What is the Fiqh of adopting a child?

Answer: In the Name of Allah, Most Compassionate, Most Merciful,

Adopting someone else's child, bringing it up, seeing to its education and training and being kind and good towards him/her is very virtuous and a commendable act. If the child is an orphan and has no support, then the reward is much more.

In a Hadith recorded by Imam al-Bukhari in his Sahih, the Messenger of Allah (Allah bless him and give him peace) said:

> "I and the guardian of the orphan will be in Paradise like this" and the Prophet (Allah bless him and give him peace) joined his index finger with his middle finger. (Sahih al-Bukhari)

Meaning that the one who looks after the orphan will be very close to the Prophet (Allah bless him and give him peace) in Paradise.

This is an extremely neglected Sunnah of our beloved Prophet (Allah bless him & give him peace), and we should definitely encourage ourselves and others towards this direction.

However, it should always be kept in mind that according to Shariah, the lineage of the adopted child does not become established with the adoptive parents. Adoption of a child has no legal effect in Shariah. The child should not be attributed except to the natural parents, and not to those who have adopted him/her.

This is a fundamental principle and ruling laid down by the Holy Qur'an. The people in the days of ignorance (Jahiliyya) used to treat an adopted child as the real one in all aspects. The Qur'an condemned this practice with the following verse:

"And He (Allah) did not make your adopted sons your sons. That is only your speech by your mouths. And Allah guides you to the right path. Call them by (the names of) their (real) fathers. It is more just in the sight of Allah." (Surah al-Ahzab, v: 4, 5)

The Messenger of Allah (Allah bless him and give him peace) adopted the Companion Zaid ibn Haritha (Allah be pleased with him), thus the other companions (Allah be pleased with them) initially referred to him as "Zaid ibn Muhammad". When the abovementioned verse of the Qur'an was revealed, they reverted to calling him "Zaid ibn Haritha".

In view of this important principle of Shariah, the following points need to be taken in to consideration:

Legal adoption is not permissible. This means that one cannot change the lineage of an adopted child and substitute the names of his real parents with adoptive parents. The child should always be attributed to the real parents so that it becomes common knowledge amongst the people who the real parents are.

If the adoptive mother breastfeeds the adopted child, then it becomes their foster child. In this case the child will be similar to the real children with regards to the Nikah and Hijab rules, i.e. the child can not marry the foster parent, neither any of the foster parent's children. However with regards to inheritance, the child will not inherit from the family.

If the adoptive mother does not breastfeed the adopted child, then the relationship of fosterage will not be established and the

37

child will be classed as other children with regards to Nikah and Hijab. An adopted child can marry its adoptive parents and their children. Also if a male child is adopted by a woman, she will have to observe Hijab from him after he reaches the age of puberty and visa versa. The adopted child will also (after puberty) observe Hijab with the adoptive parent's children.

An adopted child will not inherit from his adoptive parents and to regard an adopted child as a real child in the matter of inheritance is incorrect. However, it should be remembered that although the child cannot inherit from the adoptive parents, it is permissible, rather advisable to make a bequest in its favour in ones life time. This "will" for the child can be made up to one third of one's wealth, provided the child is not already included in the list of inheritors.

It is necessary to allow the adopted child to meet its real parents. Preventing him/her from meeting them and creating any obstacles will be considered as oppression.

Good behaviour and conduct should be displayed towards the adopted children, especially if they are orphans. If a person cannot look after the adopted child in a proper manner, then he should not adopt, otherwise he will earn punishment rather than reward.

The wealth of the adopted child, who has not yet reached puberty, should be kept safe. If there is a need to spend the money on the child, then one can utilize the child's money upon him. However it should be spent with extreme care and there should be no extravagance. Loans cannot be taken from the child's money, nor can it be given in charity.

From the foregoing, all your queries should be answered; nevertheless here are the answers to your questions:

Yes, the boy will be considered a brother to the children whose mother breastfed him, and therefore all the rules Nikah will apply.

Yes, the boy will be a Mahram to the woman who breastfed her and thus Nikah with her or her children will be not allowed.

No, the boy will not be a Mahram to the adoptive mother and will have to observe Hijab with her after reaching puberty and also the rules of Nikah will apply.

And Allah Knows Best

[Mufti] Muhammad ibn Adam

Darul Iftaa

Leicester , UK

Marriage with a Shi'a is invalid!

In conclusion, the marriage between a Shia & Sunni is invalid and here we have gathered opinions of many Sunni Scholars of different backgrounds who agree on the invalidity of such a marriage..

Marriage with a Shi'a

By Shaykh (Mufti) Muhammad Ibn Adam (HA)

Question: I have spoken to a lot of people regarding this issue please be so kind to give me the right advice. Basically please tell me the difference between Sunni and shi'a. Myself am sunni follow the Hanafi fiqh, however to cut along story short I met this guy he was shia. He proposed and then obviously I was faced with all these issues? I would just like to know your understanding of sunni shia marriages and the major differences. I have actually declined but I still need reassurance. I have read your webpage and am in agreement with all you say that's why I think you will not give me a biased view and maybe just reassure me that my decision was right!

Answer: In the Name of Allah, Most Compassionate, Most Merciful,

T he Messenger of Allah (Allah bless him & give him peace) himself explained that the primary consideration in choosing a spouse should be their Deen.

In a Hadith recorded by many Hadith scholars, the Messenger of Allah (Allah bless him & give him peace) said:

"A woman is married for four reasons, her wealth, lineage, status and Deen. Choose the one who is religious." (Sahih al-Bukhari)

This also applies to women, in that a man is married for four reasons.

"Deen" is a very comprehensive word. It does not only mean praying and fasting. Rather, it relates to one's entire conduct of life.

Therefore, it covers:

Belief (Aqidah)

Outward worship (Ibadaat)

Good character and manners (Akhlaq)

Good dealings with others (Mu'amalaat)

Turning to Allah in all affairs (Suluk)

Therefore, the first and foremost thing that should be considered before marrying someone is their religious belief and conduct of life.

With regards to marrying a Shi'a man, firstly, it should be understood that there are two types of Shi'as.

Those who hold beliefs that constitute disbelief (kufr), such as having the belief that the Qur'an has been altered, Sayyiduna Ali (Allah be pleased with him) is God, the angel Jibril made an error in descending with the revelation on the Messenger of Allah (Allah bless him & give him peace) rather than Sayyiduna Ali (Allah be pleased with him), accusing Sayyida Ai'isha (Allah be pleased with her) of committing adultery or denying the Companionship (suhba) of Sayyiduna Abu Bakr (Allah be pleased with him).

The great Hanafi jurist, Imam Ibn Abidin (Allah have mercy on him) states:

"There is no doubt in the disbelief (kufr) of those that falsely accuse Sayyida Ai'isha (Allah be pleased with her) of adultery, deny the Companionship of Sayyiduna Abu Bakr (Allah be pleased with him), believe that sayyiduna Ali (Allah be pleased with him) was God or that the angel Jibril by mistake descended with the revelation (wahi) on the Messenger of Allah (Allah bless him & give peace), etc... which is apparent Kufr and contrary to the teachings of the Qur'an." (Radd al-Muhtar, 4/453)

Therefore, Shi'as who hold such beliefs are without doubt out of the fold of Islam.

Those who do not hold beliefs that constitute Kufr, such as believing that Sayyiduna Ali (Allah be pleased with him) was the rightful first Caliph after the demise of the Messenger of Allah, belief in the twelve Imams, etc...

Such Shi'as cannot be termed as out of the fold of Islam, rather they are considered to be severely deviated and transgressors (fisq).

Imam Ibn Abidin states:

"It is difficult to make a general statement and judge all the Shi'as to be non-believers, for the scholars have agreed on the deviation and defection of the deviated sects." (ibid)

It should be remarked here that some members of the Shi'a community display outwardly not to have believes that constitute Kufr, but keep these beliefs in their heart, which they call Taqiyya.

The case with such people is that if they did hold beliefs that constitute Kufr in their heart but outwardly denied them, then even though according to Allah and in the hereafter they will be regarded as non-Muslims, but we will judge them according to their outward statements and actions.

The Messenger of Allah (Allah bless him & give him peace) is reported to have said: "I have been ordered to judge people according to their outward condition."

Keeping the above in mind, it becomes clear that marrying Shi'as that are not considered Muslims is out of the question. If one was to marry such a person, the marriage (nikah) would be invalid.

Shi'as that are not considered to be out of the fold of Islam are still regarded to be severely deviated, thus marriage with them also should never be considered, although the Nikah will be valid. This becomes more important when the case is of a Sunni Muslim girl marrying a Shi'a boy, as the affect this can have on the wife and children may be detrimental.

In conclusion, the decision you made not to marry a Shi'a boy is correct indeed. It could have long term damages with regards to your beliefs and your children's beliefs. There are many Sunni practising pious brothers you could get married to. May Allah bless you with a pious and caring husband.

And Allah Knows Best

[Mufti] Muhammad ibn Adam

Darul Iftaa

Leicester , UK

A Specific Case of Sunni-Shi'a Marriage

By Shaykh (Mufti) Muhammad Ibn Adam (HA)

Question: I am a female doctor, who follows the Hanafi Madhab, and I need your guidance in the following matter:

I wish to marry my classmate whom I know for the last 13 years (including the last 7 years since we have decided to get married). He is a Shi'a and due to this reason my parents and brothers are against this marriage. I was aware of the problems that his being Shi'a could create for me. So I tried to find as much as I could about the religious views of shia- sect, in general, from his and our books of fiqh. I then asked him directly what his beliefs were.

He does not have any such beliefs that constitute Kufr (e.g. he does not think that Hazrat Ali is god or he should have been the last prophet or that there are alterations in the Holy Quran etc.) He does however believe that Hazrat Ali should have been the first caliph, for which he gives reference of the event at Ghadir Khum. But at the same time, he has never shown any disrespect for the other 3 caliphs or Sahabah & has a personal view that if The Prophet (P.B.U.H) had declared Hazrat Ali as the first caliph in his life, it would have been an indication of bias. I have found him to be thoroughly well mannered, devoted to his profession and listens to reason and logic. I have seen that if he is convinced properly he does not keep following something blindly. He offers prayers 5 times a day, instead of combining Duhr-Asar and Maghrib- Isha prayers.

His parents share the same religious views and they added that my colleague's paternal grand mother was Sunni and remained so after her marriage. Their family has several Shia – Sunni marriages. They do not believe in self beating/using chains and knives. They have never attended Muharram processions, but they regularly attend majlis (lecture) on 9th/ 10th Muharram. They also re-assured me

that I will have complete freedom to follow my own Sunni Hanafi Madhab.

I have been trying to convince my family to agree to this marriage since 7 years. My father concerned several local religious scholars to sort out this issue. But some said that this nikkah will be valid and some said otherwise.

My brother told me about your website. He showed me a reply from you to a question regarding marriage with Shi'a. You have regarded such a nikkah to be valid, but at the same time cautioned to be careful when the matter is of marrying a sunni girl to a shia. I believe that majority of cases require an individualized approach, as I believe that not all shia are extremists or deviants. I have seen the same individualized approach in your answers regarding various issues and not just this one.

Can you please advice on whether this marriage is allowed? I put my trust in you to guide us in this matter, as I genuinely believe that Allah Has Blessed you with an objective vision and your opinion in this matter is pivotal to me and my family.

Answer: In the Name of Allah, Most Compassionate, Most Merciful,

I f it is true that he does not hold any beliefs that constitute disbelief (kufr), which include (and is not limited to) believing that the Qur'an was altered, accusing Sayyida A'isha (Allah be pleased with her) of committing adultery, denying the Companionship (suhba) of Sayyiduna Abu Bakr (Allah be pleased with him), and the other things you have mentioned in your question, then technically your marriage with him will be 'valid', meaning that the marriage contract will be recognized in Sunni law, and you will not be guilty of living in a unlawful relationship. However, if he does hold beliefs that constitute Kufr, then the marriage will not be considered valid; hence, even if you were to marry him, you will be considered living in an illicit unlawful (haram) relationship. This was explained in detail in a previous answer posted on our website titled: 'Marriage with a Shi'a'.

The Sunni position on marrying a member of the Shi'a community who does not hold beliefs that constitute Kufr is that even though the marriage may 'technically' be valid, it is still best avoided due to the many stances of Shi'as being considered as deviation by Sunni Muslims. The gravity or otherwise of taking this step also depends on the exact nature of beliefs held by the person in question.

You state that the brother whom you wish to marry believes that 'Hazrat Ali should have been the first caliph' but 'he has never shown any disrespect for the other three Caliphs or Sahaba'. This is very significant. If you can be fully assured and convinced of the fact that he has the utmost of respect and regard for all the Companions (Allah be pleased with them all), and that he considers the other three Caliphs to have a higher status than Sayyiduna Ali (Allah be pleased with him) in the order of: 1) Abu Bakr, 2) Umar, 3) Uthman, 4) Ali (Allah be pleased with them all), then I believe you may marry him.

In other words, the only differences between him and Sunni Muslims are the following:

Sayyiduna Ali (Allah be pleased with him) should have been the first Caliph of the Muslims, but this does not mean any of the other Companions (sahaba) were guilty of any wrongdoing, rather they are all forgiven by Allah, and Allah is pleased with all of them and they are all pleased with Allah. They are the highest of people after the Messenger of Allah (Allah bless him & give him peace), and the highest in Maqam is Abu Bakr, then Umar, then Uthman and then Ali (Allah be pleased with them all).

He attends lectures on the topic of the martyrdom of Sayyiduna Husayn (Allah be pleased with him) in the month of Muharram, but does not believe in self beating, etc.

Other than the above two things, if there are no issues, then you may go ahead and marry him, but it will still be somewhat disliked to do so. The reason for this is that according to the beliefs of Sunni Muslims, one who believes that Sayyiduna Ali (Allah be pleased with him) was the worthy first Caliph is also misguided. (See: Al-Aqida al-Tahawiyya with its commentaries) As such, marriage should be avoided in normal situations and whenever possible.

Another aspect worth considering is whether you will be free to practise Islam as a Sunni, and whether your children will also have a chance to be Sunni Muslims.

And Allah Knows Best

[Mufti] Muhammad ibn Adam

Darul Iftaa

Leicester , UK

Sunni girl & Shia boy

By Shaykh (Mufti) Ismail Moosa (HA)

Conclusion

In light of all the above, it is apparent that the vast majority of present-day Shia's are not Muslims. If the person in question ascribes to any of these heretic views, nikaah will NOT be permissible with him. (Imdadul Ahkaam 2/213 Maktabah Daul uloom Karachi, Khairul fatawa 1/374 Shirkat printing press, Kifaayatul Mufti 1/289 Darul ishaat, Bahishti zewar kitab an nikah) In fact, the Shia kitabs show that it's not permissible for Shias to marry sunnis, as they regard sunnis as disbelievers. "It is not permissible to marry a sunni because they are Kaafirs" (Tahdhidul Akaam, Manlaa Yahzurulul Faqih 3/258.)

If this person claims to be from the Tafdheelis (The group that are considered as Muslims), then too extreme precaution should be exercised. There is the possibility he will conceal his real beliefs and practice on taqiyyah. (Kifaayatul mufti 1/289-290 Darul ishaat) Also keep in mind the Shia practice of mutah (temporary marriage).

Bear in mind that even though it is permissible to marry the tafdheelis it is highly discouraged. (ibid) Marriage is a lifetime affair; therefore, you exercise extreme precaution. Whoever gives up something for the sake of Allaah, Allaah will compensate him with something better. We ask Allaah to make you strong and grant you a good life in this world and in the Hereafter.

And Allah knows best

Wassalam

Ml. Ismail Moosa,
Student Darul Iftaa

Checked and Approved by:

Mufti Ebrahim Desai
Darul Iftaa, Madrassah In'aamiyyah

Sunni girl loves a Shia boy

Shaykh Muhammad Aal 'Abd al-Lateef (islam-qa.com)

I need to find some useful info about shias and thier difference between us sunnis... i know this man and he loves me very much and wishes to marry me - forever not the mut aa type of marraige, however i know his bsiefs are not in line with the sunnis so i ahve discussed this wiht him and he has agreed to to research the differences - i ma hoping that this way he will be able to decide for himself which is the right path my problem is that i ma not able to find any sights whihc provide proper comparison and which do not directly accuse shias as being wwrong - i wish to talk to someone about this aaas i know there I wll be questions raised between me and this person however i need assistance and would much apreciate it if i could talk to someone or get a source where even he could study which would not make him feel as if his beiefs are being pout down - i think that telling soeone softly and nicely will amke a person more willing to listen than saying his beilefs are worng?

Praise be to Allaah.

We Sunnis wish all people well, and we ask Allaah to guide all those who are misled and to reward all those who obey Him. We hope that Allaah will guide those Raafidis...

The differences between the Ahl al-Sunnah (Sunnis) and the Raafidis are very great and are fundamental. For example, the Raafidis say that the Qur'aan was altered, and they condemn most of the Sahaabah (may Allaah be pleased with them) and think that they went astray; they exaggerate about their imaams and worship them, and give them precedence over the Prophets and angels; they go on pilgrimages to mashhads (shrines) and graves,

49

where they do all kinds of actions of shirk, associating others in worship with Allaah. They also believe in hypocrisy (as a tenet of faith) and call it taqiyah (dissimulation), and they believe in al-badaa'(the notion that Allaah "changes His mind"), al-raj'ah (the Return, i.e., the raising of the dead to life again for some time in the same form as they were before) and absolute infallibility of their imaams, and in prostrating on a handful of clay...

We advise you to read "Al-Khutoot al-'Areedah" by Muhibb al-Deen al-Khateeb [this book is available in English – Translator], or Mukhtasar al-Tuhfat al-Ithna' 'Ashariyyah by al-Dahlawi, or Fikrat al-Taqreeb bayna Ahl al-Sunnah wa'l-Shee'ah by Naasir al-Qaffaari.

And we advise you not to think of marrying this man... Whoever gives up something for the sake of Allaah, Allaah will compensate him with something better. We ask Allaah to make you strong and grant you a good life in this world and in the Hereafter.

We would also remind you that it is not permitted to have relationships with non-mahram men, as you will find explained clearly in Questions 2005 , 9465 And 1114 We ask Allaah to help you to do all that is good.

Contraception, Morning after and IVF

First of all, it should be known that, one of the main aims of marriage in Islam is procreation. Islam encourages its followers to reproduce in large numbers in order to increase the size of the Ummah of our Prophet (Allah bless him & give him peace).

Birth Control & Contraception

Which method of contraception suits me? (NHS)

By Shaykh (Mufti) Muhammad Ibn Adam (HA)

Question: What is the Islamic verdict on contraception and birth control in general? Is it only permissible at times of need?

Answer: In the Name of Allah, Most Compassionate, Most Merciful,

First of all, it should be known that, one of the main aims of marriage in Islam is procreation. Islam encourages its followers to reproduce in large numbers in order to increase the size of the Ummah of our Prophet (Allah bless him & give him peace).
Allah Most High says in the Qur'an:

"So now hold intercourse with your wives and seek (the children) what Allah has ordained for you." (Surah al-Baqarah, V: 187)

In a Hadith recorded by Imam Abu Dawud, Imam an-Nasa'i and others, the Messenger of Allah (Allah bless him and give him peace) said:

> "Marry women who are loving and reproduce in abundance, for I shall outnumber the other nations by you."

It is clear from the above, that Shariah encourages its followers to abstain from practicing birth control, especially, when it is given a formal, organized and general approach. Therefore, one should refrain from practicing contraception unless necessary.

As far as the Shar'i ruling is concerned, there are two categories of birth control and the ruling of each is different. The ruling of each category is as follows:

Permanent Irreversible Contraception

This type of contraception is carried out when the couple decide never to have a baby. It is done with a sterilization operation carried out either on the man (Vasectomy) or the woman (Tubectomy) and renders the couple incapable of ever having children.

The ruling with regards to this is that, it is unlawful (Haram) to carry out such operations. There are many Narrations of the Messenger of Allah (Allah bless him & give him peace) and clear texts of the Fuqaha (Jurists) which determine this.

The Companion, Sayyiduna Abdullah ibn Mas'ud (Allah be pleased with him) said:

> "We use engage in Jihad in the company of the Messenger of Allah (Allah bless him & give him peace) and our wives did not accompany us. We said: O Prophet of Allah! Shall we not castrate ourselves? He forbade us from doing so." (Sahih al-Bukhari)

The great Hanafi Jurist, Allama Ibn Abidin (Allah have mercy on him) says:

> "Castration of humans is Haram." (Radd al-Muhtar).

Imam al-Ayni (Allah have mercy on him) says:

"Castration (and sterilization, m) is prohibited with the consensus of all the scholars." (Umdat al-Qari)

However, in cases of extreme necessity, Irreversible contraception will become permissible. For example, a woman's life is in danger or repeated pregnancies gravely damage her health, etc. This however, should be advised by a Muslim qualified doctor.

Temporary Reversible Contraception

There are many methods by which reversible contraception can be performed. Coitus interruptus (Withdrawal method), the pill, using of the condom, i.u.d, spermicidal, just to mention a few.

The ruling on reversible contraception is that, it is somewhat disliked (makruh tanzihan) if practiced without any reason. If there is a genuine reason, then it will be totally permissible with the permission of the wife. Some of the reasons (for the permissibility of reversible contraception), which the Fuqaha mention, are:

Physical state of the woman,

Weakness and illness,

The couple are on a distant journey,

The couple's relations are unstable and divorce is likely,

Spacing out children in order to give them adequate care and attention,

If contraception is practiced due to a reason contrary to the teachings of Shariah, then it will not be permissible. Some of these reasons are:

Fear of poverty and not being able to provide,

For the fashion of keeping small families and imitating the Kuffar,

Being ashamed of having a girl,

There are many narrations from the Messenger of Allah (Allah bless him and give him peace) which signify the permissibility of reversible contraception, but at the same time indicate it to be undesirable.

Sayyiduna Jabir (Allah be pleased with him) says:

"We used to practice Coitus interruptus (Withdrawal method) while the Qur'an was being revealed. The Messenger of Allah (Allah bless him & give him peace) knew of this and did not prohibit us." (Sahih al-Bukhari and Sahih Muslim)

This has more or less been mentioned by the scholars in their books. (See Imam Nawawi in his commentary of Sahih Muslim, Mulla Ali al-Qari in al-Mirqat, Ibn Abidin in his Radd al-Muhtar and others.

For more details, please refer to my book on this subject titled Birth Control and Abortion (Revised Edition), available from the Darul Iftaa, Leicester, UK.

And Allah Knows Best

[Mufti] Muhammad ibn Adam

Darul Iftaa

Leicester , UK

The Morning-After Pill

By Shaykh (Mufti) Muhammad Ibn Adam (HA)

Question: I have been under the impression that in Islam it is forbidden to use the morning after pill as it is an abortive method of birth control. A friend recently argued that it was not, and that it is permissible to use it. Could you please provide a detailed response as to what the majority of scholars say regarding this issue?

Answer: In the Name of Allah, Most Compassionate, Most Merciful,

The Morning-after pill (emergency contraception) is estimated to prevent about 85% of pregnancies. It is thought to work by:

Stopping the ovaries from releasing an egg,

Preventing sperm from fertilizing any egg that may have already been released; or, (importantly)

Stopping a fertilized egg from attaching itself into the womb lining. (See: The official brochure of Schering Health Care Limited, manufacturers of Levonelle pills).

Other experts state:

"Popularly dubbed the morning-after pill, the drug Levonelle can actually be taken up to 72 hours after intercourse. The 1861 Offences against the Person Act prohibits the supply of any "poison or other noxious thing" with intent to cause miscarriage. SPUC's argument is based on the fact that the drug stops an embryo from implanting in the lining of the womb. The organisation successfully applied last year for leave to bring a judicial review of the government's decision to reclassify the drug as suitable for over-the-counter sale. The court will be asked to consider "what is the precise moment at which a woman becomes pregnant." Is it when the egg is fertilized, or when the resulting embryo is implanted in the womb? If it is the former, then the court could rule that emergency contraception causes a miscarriage and is illegal."

From an Islamic perspective, temporary contraception is permitted in cases of individual needs as explained in earlier posts. The various methods of temporary and reversible contraception prevent the sperm from fertilizing the egg, hence they are permitted. However, if a particular method was to expel the fertilized ovum and prevent it from attaching itself into the womb lining, then the ruling would be somewhat different.

Shaykh Taqi Usmani (may Allah preserve him) states whilst discussing the employment of a loop as a means of contraception:

"In the first case where the loop acts as a preventive measure against fertilization, it is similar to any other contraceptive and the rules regarding al-Azl (withdrawal method & temporary contraception in general) may be applied to the loop also, i.e. its use is permissible in Shariah in cases of individual needs, like the sickness or the weakness of the woman where pregnancy may endanger her health.

In the second case, however, (when fertilization takes place, and the fertilized ovum is expelled from the uterus by the loop), the rules of al-Azl cannot be applied, because in that case it is not merely a preventive measure; rather, it expels the fertilized ovum from the uterus after conception. Therefore, it acts as a device to effect an abortion. Hence, the rules of abortion shall apply....As the loop expels the fertilized ovum within two weeks, its use cannot be held as prohibited totally. However, being a device of abortion, its use is not advisable and it should be restricted to the cases of the real medical needs only." (Contemporary Fatawa, P: 136-137)

In light of the above Fatwa, it becomes clear that if a reversible contraceptive device acts after the sperm has fertilized the egg and the device merely prevents a fertilized egg from implanting itself into the womb lining, then the ruling on employing such a

56

contraceptive device would be different. The ruling on such contraceptive devices would be similar to that of carrying out an abortion at an earlier stage, which is impermissible unless there is a genuine and valid reason.

Therefore, the morning-after pill will have the same ruling as the loop, for it may work by stopping a fertilized egg from attaching itself into the womb, as mentioned above.. Thus, the rules of an early abortion would apply in this case also; and hence it should only be used in extreme medical conditions.

In conclusion, the ruling on employing the loop, the morning-after pill or any other method that may act after the egg has been fertilized as a means of contraception is somewhat different to the general ruling on reversible contraception (al-Azl). Reversible contraception is generally permitted if practised on an individual level, whilst employing any method that may prevent a fertilized egg from implanting itself into the womb will not be allowed except in certain medical conditions, for which one should consult a reliable scholar of knowledge and piety.

Selling the morning-after pill

As far as selling the morning after pill is concerned, one should keep in mind the juristic (fiqhi) principle which states:

"Everything that it is possible to use in a permitted manner is lawful to sell" (See: Radd al-Muhtar, 6/391)

Hence, it would be permitted (halal) to sell the various types of contraceptives including the morning-after pill, as they have legally permissible uses. The morning-after pill (as explained earlier) can be used in cases of medical need; hence, it would be permitted to sell it. It is analogous to selling a knife, in that one may use it to cut a fruit, but unfortunately it could be used to stab someone.

Thereafter, if it does end up being used unlawfully, the seller will not share the sin or blame, because that unlawful action was purely through the deliberate wilful action of the purchaser, not because of one's selling. One does not even need to ask or investigate about why it is being used. Assume it is a lawful use.

However, if in a particular case, the seller was certain of it being used unlawfully, it would best be to avoid selling it to that particular individual.

(Based primarily on my soon to be published work (Insha Allah) Birth Control and Abortion (Revised Edition), from www.whitethreadpress.com)

And Allah Knows Best

[Mufti] Muhammad ibn Adam

Darul Iftaa

Leicester , UK

Permanent Contraception (Female Sterilisation) - Does Intention affect Permissibility?

By Shaykh (Mufti) Muhammad Ibn Adam (HA)

Question:A 26 year old woman presented to a general gynaecology clinic requesting sterilisation. She worked as the manager of a large legal practice in London. She had never been pregnant. She was five years married and her husband used condoms for contraception. At the age of 17 she had discovered that she had a serious congenital heart defect. Neither she nor her husband had any desire to have children, and they had spoken about this at some length. The reasons she gave for requesting sterilisation were that she had no desire to have children and did not have faith in other forms of contraception (and did not wish to change her lifestyle or threaten her financial status; she saw children as a financial burden; felt that children would prohibit many important life choices, including the opportunity to travel; thought the world was already burdened with enough people; and had serious anxieties about the risk of medical complications during a pregnancy as her cardiologist had told her that pregnancy would be risky). The gynaecologist suggested alternative and reversible methods of contraception, including the intrauterine progestogen system. He also asked whether her partner would consider vasectomy. He explained the risks of laparoscopic sterilisation, which include a small risk of death and a risk of about 1 in 300 of requiring an emergency laparotomy to repair damage done to internal organs. The patient declined the intrauterine system and refused to ask her husband to have a vasectomy as he was only 25. She explained that, should she die prematurely, her husband might meet a new partner who wanted to have children.

Is her request for sterilisation permissible (Islamically, whether she is Muslim or not)?

Is the doctor allowed to carry out this procedure? (muslimah doctor)

Would the ruling change if her main reason for requesting a sterilisation was not that she did not want children, but that it might be risky with her given congenital heart condition (medical reason)? I.e. docs her intention matter, whether she doesn't want a child (against God's will?) or whether she wished to preserve her own health (conforming to God's will for medical reasons?)

If sterilisation is permissible in any of the cases, is the husband's permission required? (E.g. in 'azl, it is generally with mutual consent... can sterilisation be viewed Islamically as permanent 'azl?)

Hypothetically, if there was a 100% fool-proof method of contraception that was temporary (i.e. not sterilisation, so no defacing or altering the creation of Allah (swt), then would this form of contraception be allowed given that possibility of conceiving with the contraceptive is absolutely zero?

Answer: In the Name of Allah, Most Compassionate, Most Merciful,

Under normal circumstances, female sterilization is considered to be absolutely and decidedly prohibited (haram) in Shari'ah. The irreversible nature associated with both the male and female sterilizations clearly contradicts one of the primary purposes (maqasid) of marriage which is to have children, as mentioned by Imam Abu Hamid al-Ghazali in his *Ihya' Ulum al-Din*.

Furthermore, sterilization is a form of mutilation of one's body (muthla), which has been clearly forbidden in the Shari'ah. Allah Most High mentions in al-Nisa' the words of Satan, when he said:

"I will mislead them, and I will create in them false desires; I will order them to slit the ears of cattle and to deface the (fair) nature created by Allah."

However, in cases of absolute necessity, sterilization does become permitted. The well-known principle of Islamic jurisprudence based on the guidelines of the Qur'an and Sunna states:

"Necessities make prohibitions lawful." (Ibn Nujaym, Al-Ashbah wa al-Naza'ir 85)

Cases of absolute necessity include a woman's life or her permanent health being severely threatened by pregnancy, or her facing the risk of losing her life with additional births after having gone through Caesarean operations on previous occasions. As such, if unbiased and professional medical advice is taken, and one comes to the conclusion that the life or permanent health of a woman would be seriously affected by pregnancy and that there is no other cure for her illness, only then would female sterilization be permitted.

You state that the woman in question has a serious congenital heart condition and as such her becoming pregnant might be risky. In light of the above explanation, she will need to obtain professional medical advice ideally from an experienced and upright Muslim doctor (who knows the severity of the prohibition of sterilization in Islam) and then act accordingly. If the medical expert feels that pregnancy is a severe risk to her life or permanent health, then she may undergo sterilization.

The other reasons outlined in your question do not justify sterilization. In fact, some - such as seeing children as a financial burden thus fearing poverty and thinking that the world was already burdened with enough people - are in direct conflict with the teachings of Islam. Even reversible contraception is not permitted due to "such" reasons and intentions in mind.

As for the doctor and medical practitioner, if sterilization is justified (in light of the above-mentioned explanation), then it is permitted to carry out the operation on the patient. If, however, it is not Islamically justified, such as when there is no absolute necessity, or when alternatives are available, then it is not permitted for the Muslim doctor to perform the operation, since this would be held as assisting another in a sinful act.

And Allah Knows Best

[Mufti] Muhammad ibn Adam, Darul Iftaa, Leicester , UK

IVF & Surrogate Motherhood

What happens during IVF? (NHS)

By Shaykh (Mufti) Muhammad Ibn Adam (HA)

Question: What is the Islamic position on surrogate motherhood, which involves "a woman who becomes pregnant usually by artificial insemination or surgical implantation of a fertilized egg for the purpose of carrying the fetus to term for another woman"?

Answer: In the Name of Allah, Most Compassionate, Most Merciful,

The problem of infertility is a very old problem and has always been a matter of concern for human beings. From the very early times, people have tried to treat this problem with all kinds of treatments and therapies. Infertility is defined as the failure to produce viable pregnancy within one year of regular sexual intercourse, without the use of contraceptives of course.

Islam teaches us that the creation of life is the exclusive function of Allah Most High. No matter what method and means one employs, if Allah Almighty does not wish to grant children, one will never have children.

Allah Most High says:

> To Allah belongs the dominion of the heavens and the earth. He creates what He wills. He bestows female (children) to whomsoever He wills and bestows male (children) to whomsoever He wills, or He bestows both males and females, and He leaves barren whomsoever He wills. He is full of Knowledge and Power. (Surah al-Shura, V. 49-50)

Sayyiduna Abu Said al-Khudri (may Allah be pleased with him) narrates that the Messenger of Allah (Allah bless him & give him peace) was asked about coitus interruptus (azl) whereupon he said: The child is not born from all the liquid (sperm) and when Allah intends to create something, nothing can prevent Him. (Sahih Muslim, no. 1438)

Thus, the granting of children is the exclusive right and function of Allah Most High. Hence a Muslim should always first resort to supplicating Allah Most High, for if He wills to grant and bestow children, none can prevent Him.

The Quran mentions two great Prophets of Allah who were also faced with this problem, but supplicated and beseeched Allah Most High, and were granted children in their old age.

Allah Most High says regarding Sayyiduna Zakariyya (peace be upon him):

There did Zakariyya pray to his Lord, saying: O my Lord! Grant unto me from You a progeny that is pure: for surely You are the Hearer of prayer. Then, while he was standing in prayer in the chamber, the angels called unto him: (Allah) gives you glad tidings of Yahya, witnessing the truth of a Word from Allah, a leader and chaste, and a Prophet, from amongst the righteous. He said: O my lord! How shall I have a son seeing I am very old and my wife is barren? Allah said: So it shall be, Allah does what He wills. (Surah Al Imran, V. 39-40)

Sayyiduna Zakariyya (peace be upon him), despite being very old did not hesitate for a moment in supplicating and asking Allah Most High to grant him children. It is reported from Sayyiduna Ibn Abbas (Allah be pleased with him) that on the day Sayyiduna Zakariyya (peace be upon him) was given the glad tidings of Sayyiduna Yahyas birth, he was 120 years of age and his wife was 98. (See: Tafsir al-Kabir of Imam al-Razi, 3/214

In another place of the Qur'an, Allah Most High says regarding Sayyiduna Ibrahim (peace and blessings be upon him):

> And his wife was standing (there), and she laughed: And We gave her glad tidings of Ishaq, and after him, of Yaqub. She said: Alas for me! Shall I bear a child, seeing I am an old woman, and my husband here is an old man? That would indeed be a wonderful thing! (Surah Hud, V. 71-72)

> This great Prophet of Allah, Sayyiduna Ibrahim (peace be upon him) was also 120 years of age, whilst his wife Sayyida Sarah (peace be upon her) was 90 or 98 years old. (Tafsir Abi Saud, 4/325). Despite this, they were given the glad tidings of not only a child but also a grandchild.

Therefore, the first step to be taken is to beseech Allah Most High and ask from Him, for if He wills, one will be bestowed with children, and if he does not desire, nothing can bring about children.

One may also resort to adopting children. However, one must remember that there are strict rules with regards to adopting a child. The child cannot be attributed except to his real parents. If the problem is with the wife, the husband may also marry a second time, but here also, there are strict conditions and rules that need to be met.

Alternatively, the couple may resort to medical treatment. When undertaking medical treatment, one must remember that means themselves do not have an effect. It is only through the mercy of Allah that one will be granted children.

Modern advancement in medical science has come forth with many methods in treating infertility. At times, the husbands sperm is artificially inseminated into the wifes uterus (AIH). Sometimes a third persons (donor) sperm is introduced into the wifes uterus (AID), or it is mixed with the husbands sperm and then artificially inseminated (AIM).

Another method is of fertilizing the womans eggs in a laboratory test tube with the husbands or a donors sperm and then returning the resulting ovum into the womans uterus. This method is known as In-vitro fertilization (IVF).

Surrogate motherhood is also a method in treating infertility. It involves using the service of another woman to serve as a carrier for the ovum of the couple. The woman makes her self available to inject the fertilized ovum into her own womb and then carries the child to its full term on behalf of the other couple.

People resort to this procedure either because a married woman who desires to have a child has a problem in carrying the child to its full term, or because of her desire to simply forgo the trouble of conception and labour.

As far as the Islamic ruling on these various forms and methods of treatment is concerned, one must keep in mind a very important principle, for that answers all the questions. The principle is that resorting to these methods of medical treatment is permissible as long as only the husband and wife are involved. It is completely unlawful to use a third partys (donor) sperm or eggs.

The reason being is that Islam has completely prohibited adultery (zina) and everything that leads to it. Islam lays allot of importance on the preservation of lineage. The preservation of lineage (hifz al-nasl) is one of the five universals and objectives of Shariah. As such, introducing a third party into the family equation would confuse the lineage, hence it will not be allowed. Using the sperm or eggs of a third person would create doubt and confusion with regards to the childs identity. The childs lineage and identity will not be preserved and safeguarded.

Many contemporary scholars have declared the introduction of other than the husbands sperm into the wife akin to adultery (zina), hence a major sin. They state that artificial insemination of other than the husbands sperm and adultery are both similar in effect; that is, in both cases the tillage is inseminated by a stranger. It is also a more severe crime than legal adoption, which is also completely prohibited in Shariah.

Allah Most High says:

And those who guard their private parts. Except with those joined to them in the marriage bond, or (the captives) whom their right hands possess, for (in their case) they are free from blame. But those whose desires exceed those limits are transgressors. (Surah al-Muminun, V. 5-7)

Ruwayfi ibn Thabit al-Ansari (Allah be pleased with him) narrates that the Messenger of Allah (Allah bless him & give him peace) said on the day of Hunayn:

> It is unlawful for a man who believes in Allah and the last day that he waters the plant of another. (Sunan Abu Dawud, no. 2151 & Sunan Tirmidhi)

The meaning of watering the plant of another is to introduce ones sperm into the womb of another persons wife.

Therefore, all forms of treatment in which a third party is involved are completely unlawful. Hence, AID, AIM and surrogate motherhood is out of the question.

Moreover, the question of to whom will the child be attributed also arises in such cases. Scholars mention that despite the prohibition of resorting to such methods, if one did employ them, the child will always be attributed to the mothers husband.

> There is a famous Hadith recorded by Imam Muslim and others in which the Messenger of Allah (Allah bless him and give him peace) said: The child will be attributed to the husband and the adulterer will receive the stone. The meaning of this Hadith is that the right of paternity will always be for the person who is married to the childs mother.

Thus, if a donors sperm or the husbands sperm mixed with that of a donor was introduced into the wife, the child will still be attributed to the husband. However, if the husband refuses to accept the child as his own, it will only be attributed to the mother.

If an unmarried woman was artificially inseminated with the sperm of another man, the child will only be attributed to herself. The man whose sperm was used will have nothing to do with the child.

In the case of surrogate motherhood, the problem becomes even more perplexing as to who will be considered the childs real mother? Is it the woman who provided eggs from which the child is born, or is it the one whose womb serves as a carrier for the child and then gives birth?

Many contemporary scholars have stated that based on the Quranic verse which states: Their mothers are only those who gave them birth (Surah al-Mujadalah, V. 2), the woman who carries the child to its full term and then gives birth to it will be considered the real mother. Hence, the woman whose eggs were used will not even be regarded as the real mother of the child. When the surrogate mother is considered to be the real mother, her husband (in light of the above mentioned Hadith) will be the father of the child unless he rejects the child, in which case the child will only be attributed to the surrogate mother.

one must also remember that it will be unlawful for a woman to use her ex-husbands frozen sperm after his death or divorce, for her marriage is terminated and her ex-husband is considered to be a stranger.

Artificial insemination between the husband and wife

As far as artificial insemination between legally married husband and wife is concerned, majority of the contemporary scholars are of the view that this is permissible. It is allowed whether the sperm of the husband is artificially inseminated and injected into the uterus of the wife, or whether the sperm of the husband and the eggs of the wife are artificially fertilized in a test tube and then inserted into the womb of the wife.

Some scholars have raised certain objections to the permissibility of artificial insemination, even if it be between married couples. They state that there are two problems Islamically in carrying out such methods.

Firstly, the sperm of the husband is normally acquired by masturbation, which is prohibited except in certain dire situations. Hence, in order to treat infertility, one will have to undergo something which is unlawful. They state that infertility is not an extreme medical problem to the extent that it would make unlawful medication lawful.

Secondly, the husband and wife both will have to expose their nakedness (awra) in order to receive treatment, and again, this is not allowed merely in order to have children, they say. Exposing of the Awra becomes permissible only in certain situations of need and necessity.

The answer to both these objections is that the desire of having children is very serious indeed. Those who are unable to bear children at times undergo depression and emotional trauma. At times, it may even lead one to infidelity and adultery. Hence, this is a case of need (dharura) wherein the rules become somewhat relaxed. Therefore, masturbation in order to obtain the sperm of the husband and exposing of the nakedness (awra) would become permissible in treating infertility.

It is analogous to circumcising an adult who accepts Islam. Carrying out a circumcision is a Sunnah, yet it is permitted (according to the majority of the scholars) for an adult man who accepts Islam to expose his nakedness (awra).

Moreover, in the case of masturbation, the idea is not to waste the sperm, rather the opposite. The sperm is used in order to impregnate the woman, whereas normally in masturbation the sperm is wasted. Also, mutual masturbation between the husband and wife is allowed, hence the wife may obtain the sperm of her husband.

One should remember here that some scholars have stipulated a condition, which is that one should be treated by someone of the same gender. Hence, the female should be treated by a female doctor at the time of obtaining her eggs and also when inserting the fertilized ovum into her womb. The husband should also be treated by a male doctor in acquiring his sperm.

In conclusion, there are three conditions for the permissibility of resorting to the various forms of treating infertility:

It must take place only between the husband and wife. There should be no third party involvement in any shape or form.

The husband and wife should be treated by someone of their own gender.

One must be extremely cautious in that there is no ambiguity in the sperm being only of the husband.

The international Islamic Fiqh academy based in Jeddah (Majma al-Fiqh al-Islami) which consists of a number of major scholars from around the globe researched this issue in October 1986, and after extensive research issued the following verdicts: Below is the translation of the Arabic text published in the academys resolutions:

Resolution No. 16(4-3)

Concerning Test Tube Babies

The Council of the Islamic Fiqh Academy holding its third session, in Amman, Hashemite Kingdom of Jordan, From 8 to 13 Safar 1407 H (11 to 16 October 1986), after having reviewed the studies on the subject of Artificial insemination and having listened to the experts and physicians, and after investigation, It became evident to the Council that there are seven (7) known methods, used nowadays, for artificial insemination:

Hence, the council decided on the following:

Firstly, the following five (5) methods are all Islamically forbidden and absolutely prohibited for its own sake or due to the consequences manifested in employing them of the lineage being confused and loss of motherhood and other Shariah prohibited matters. These methods are:

The fertilization taking place between the sperm taken from the husband and the eggs taken from a woman who is not his wife, and then the fertilized ovum being implanted into the womb of his wife.

The fertilization taking place between the sperm taken from a man who is not the husband and the eggs taken from the wife, and then the fertilized ovum being implanted into the womb of the wife.

The fertilization taking place in-vitro between the sperm and the eggs taken from the spouses, and then the fertilized ovum being implanted into the womb of a volunteer woman (i.e. surrogate motherhood).

69

The fertilization taking place in-vitro between the sperm of a man and eggs of a woman who are both strangers to one another, and then the fertilized ovum being implanted into the womb of another mans wife.

The fertilization taking place in-vitro between the sperm and the eggs taken from the spouses, and then the fertilized ovum is implanted into the womb of the husbands other wife.

Secondly, there is no problem in resorting to the sixth or seventh method, in case of necessity, provided all required precautions are taken. These two methods are:

The sperm of the husband and the eggs of the wife are taken and fertilized in-vitro, and then the fertilized ovum is implanted into the womb of the wife.

Artificial insemination, by taking the sperm of the husband and inserting it in the appropriate place of his wifes womb, for fertilization. (See: Qararat wa tawsiyyat Majma al-Fiqh al-Islami, P. 34-35)

And Allah Knows Best

[Mufti] Muhammad ibn Adam

Darul Iftaa

Leicester , UK

Welcoming a Child

Birth of a child is one of the most joyous occasions for the family, friends and the loved ones as the little bundle of joy lifts up spirits and brings endless blessings and bliss to everyone concerned.

Birth of a child is one of the most joyous occasions for the family, friends and the loved ones as the little bundle of joy lifts up spirits and brings endless blessings and bliss to everyone concerned. However it is a also a time of great responsibility for the parents to ensure that the injunctions in the Qur'aan & Sunnah are followed to ensure the blessings of Allah (SWT) for the little bundle of joy and the whole family.

Choosing the right partner:

Preparation for welcoming a child actually begins before the birth. In Islam the man or the woman is encouraged to take a "pious and practising" partner to ensure that their attention remains focused on the life hereafter and on fostering and strengthening their relationship with Allah (SWT). A man blessed with a pious Muslimah as his life partner is told to be in possession of the best of this world:

Sayyidina Abdullah Ibn Amr (RA) reported Allah's Messenger (Sallaho Alaihe Wassallam) as saying: The whole world is a provision, and the best object of benefit of the world is the pious woman. [Muslim]

Furthermore a Muslim man is encouraged to marry Muslimahs who not only pious and practising but also loving and prolific.

Sayyidina Ma'qil ibn Yasar (RA) narrated that a man came to the Prophet (Sallaho Alaihe Wassallam) and said: I have found a woman of rank and beauty, but she does not give birth to children. Should I marry her? He (Sallaho Alaihe Wassallam) said: No. He came again to him, but he (Sallaho Alaihe Wassallam)

71

prohibited him. He came to him third time, and he (the Prophet (Sallaho Alaihe Wassallam)) said: Marry women who are loving and very prolific, for I shall outnumber the peoples by you. [Abi Dawud]

Actions during Pregnancy and childbirth:

There are no specific duas or verses of the Qur'aan to be recited during pregnancy or childbirth but in general any Adhkaar, recitation of the Qur'aan can be adopted with abundant duas for the well being of the mother and the baby. The mother should make an intention that she will devote the baby for the Service of the Deen of Allah (SWT) as per the dua of wife of Imran:

[3:35] (Remember) when Imran's wife said: .O my Lord, I have vowed that what is in my womb will be devoted exclusively for You. So, accept (it) from me. You, certainly You, are the All-Hearing, the All-Knowing.

During the pangs of childbirth, certain Ulamah have recommended Surah Yaseen (Chapter 36) and other Adhkaar to ease childbirth (as incantations) and there is no prohibition in reciting them for the ease, comfort and consolation of the expectant mother.

First cry of the baby:

Generally, a baby will cry when its born and this is due to the pricking of the Shaytaan. It is encouraged to seek the protection of Allah (SWT) from Shaytaan (the Accursed) for the child:

Sayyidina Abu Huraira (RA) said, "The Prophet (Sallaho Alaihe Wassallam) said, 'No child is born but that, Satan touches it when it is born where upon it starts crying loudly because of being touched by Satan, except Mary and her Son." Abu Huraira then said, "Recite, it you wish: "And I seek Refuge with You (Allah) for her and her offspring from Satan, the outcast." (3.36) [Bukhari]

Calling the Adhan in baby's right ear:

It is from the Sunnah to hold the baby and gently call the Adhan into the right ear.

Sayyidina Abu Raafi' (RA) said, "I saw the Prophet (Sallaho Alaihe Wassallam) give the adhaan for prayer in the ear of Hussain Ibn Ali (RA) after his mother Sayyida Fatima (RA) gave birth to him," [Tirmidhi]

Iqamah in baby's left ear:

It is Mustahab (preferable) call the Iqamah (for prayers) in the left ear of the baby. Although, the evidence of this action is weak it has substantiation from the practise of early Muslims and Al-Hafidh Ibn Qayyim (HA) also quotes this practise in Tuhfat al-Mawdud bi-Ahkam al-Mawlud and lists 3 Ahadeeth (of varying authenticity).

Tahneek for the baby:

It is from the Sunnah to then soften a tiny piece of date or something sweet and to rub the lightly place it in the mouth of the baby

Sayyia A'isha (RA), the wife of the Apostle (Sallaho Alaihe Wassallam) said: Babies were brought to the Messenger of Allah (may peace be upon him) and he blessed them, and after having chewed (something, e. g. dates or any other sweet thing) he rubbed there with their soft palates. A baby was brought to him and he passed water over him (over his garment), so he asked water to be brought and sprinkled it, but he did not wash it. [Muslim]

Giving the baby a good name:

The child will be called and identified by his or her name not only in this lifetime but also in the hereafter so it is of utmost importance that a good name is given:

Sayydina Abu-Darda (RA) narrated that the Prophet (Sallaho Alaihe Wassallam) said: On the Day of Resurrection you will be called by your names and by your father's names, so give yourselves good names. [Abi Dawud]

Any name with a good meaning is permissible and it is not a requirement to give the child an Arabic name but for boys it is recommended to give the names of Allah (SWT) or names of the prophets.

Sayyidina Ibn Umar (RA) reported that Allah's Messenger (Sallaho Alaihe Wassallam) said: The names dearest to Allah are 'Abdullah and 'Abd al-Rahman. (Muslim)

Sayyidina Abu Musa (RA) narrated :I got a son and I took him to the Prophet (Sallaho Alaihe Wassallam) who named him Ibrahim, and put in his mouth the juice of a date fruit (which be himself had chewed, and invoked for Allah's blessing upon him, and then gave him back to me. He was the eldest son of Abu Musa. [Muslim]

Giving a good name on the 7th day:

A child can be named on any day but it is reported that Sayyidina Rasul-ullah (Sallaho Alaihe Wassallam) named his grandchildren on the 7th day so Muslims are encouraged to follow this noble practise and also name their child on the seventh day.

It was reported that Sayyida 'Aa'ishah (RA) said: the Messenger of Allah (Sallaho Alaihe Wassallam) did 'aqeeqah for Hasan and Hussain on the seventh day, and gave them their names. [Ibn Hiban, Hakim]

Aqeeqah on the 7th day:

Aqeeqah (sacrifice) is a noble Sunnah to remove harm from the baby.

Sayyidina Salman bin 'Amir (RA) reported that Allaah's Messenger (Sallaho Alaihe Wassallam) said: A 'qeeqah is prescribed for every child. Thus shed blood on his behalf; and remove the harmful thing from him. [Tirmidhi]

It is also from the noble Sunnah to sacrifice 2 animals for a boy and one animal for a girl on the 7th day with the intention of Aqeeqah.

Sayyidah 'Aa'ishah (RA)reported that Allah's Messenger (Sallaho Alaihe Wassallam) said: (The 'aqeeqah is) two [equivalent] sheep for the male child, and one for the female. [There is no harm whether they be male or female animals.] [Ahmed]

Feasting and distributing Aqeeqah meat:

It is recommended for a person to feast and also share the meat with family, friends and loved ones and also distribute some of it to others.

Sayyidah 'Aa'ishah (RA) said concerning the meat of the 'aqeeqah: "It should be cut into pieces, then eaten and given to others." [Ibn Abi Shaybah]

It was narrated that Sayyidina Ibn Seereen (RA) and Sayyidina Hasan al-Basri (RA) said: "Among them the 'aqeeqah was dealt with like a sacrifice; some would be eaten and some given to others." [Ibn Abi Shaybah]

Shaving the head on the 7th day:

Then it is from the Sunnah to shave the head of the child and it is preferred to start the shaving from the right hand side.

Sayyidina Samurah ibn Jundub narrated : The Prophet (Sallaho Alaihe Wassallam) said: A boy is in pledge for his Aqiqah, Sacrifice is made for him on the seventh day, his head is shaved and he is given name. [Abi Dawud]

Sayyidina Anas ibn Malik (RA) reported that Allah's Messenger (Sallaho Alaihe Wassallam) came to Mina; he went to the Jamra and threw pebbles at it, after which he went to his lodging in Mina, and sacrificed the animal. He then called for a barber and, turning his right side to him, let him shave him; after which he tiimed his left side. He then gave (these hair) to the people. [Muslim]

Giving the weight of the hair (in Silver) in Charity:

Charity equivalent to the weight of the baby' hair (in silver) should be distributed.

Sayyidina Abu Raafi' (RA) reported: "When Faatimah (R) gave birth to Hasan (RA), she asked Allaah's Messenger (Sallaho Alaihe Wassallam), 'Shouldn't I sacrifice blood (as 'aqeeqah) for my son?' He replied: No! Just shave the hair of his head, and give sadaqah (charity) equivalent to its weight in silver. She did that; and when al-Husayn was born, she did the same." [Ahmed]

Circumcision:

It is from the noble Sunnah to circumcise the boy but there is no set day or age for the procedure. Whenever it is felt that the child is healthy enough, he should be circumcised.

Sayyidina Abu Huraira (RA) narrated: The Messenger of Allaah (Sallaho Alaihe Wassallam) said: "The fitrah is five things, or five things are part of the fitrah: circumcision, shaving the pubic hairs, plucking the armpit hairs, clipping the nails and trimming the moustache." [Bukhari]

Islamic upbringing & looking after children

Bringing a child into this world is a serious responsibility and Islam attributes great importance and value to this noble cause. Parents are reminded of ensuring that the upbringing of the child conforms of the tenants of Islamic Shariah and warned of the consequences should they to slacken up in meeting their obligations and fulfilling their responsibilities.

[66:6] O you who believe, save yourselves and your families from a fire, the fuel of which is human beings and stones, appointed on which are angels, stern and severe, who do not disobey Allah in what He orders them, and do whatever they are ordered to do.

It was narrated from 'Sayydina Abd-Allaah (RA) that the Messenger of Allaah (Sallaho Alaihe Wassallam) said: "Each of you is a shepherd and is responsible for his flock. The ruler who is in charge of people is a shepherd and is responsible for them. The man is the shepherd of his household and is responsible for them. The woman is the shepherd of her husband's house and child and is responsible for them. The slave is the shepherd of his master's wealth and is responsible for it. Each of you is a shepherd and each of you is responsible for his flock." [Bukhari]

Giving good council and advice

Part of good parenting is to give good advice and to steer the child in the right direction. This practise is specially noted in the Qur'aan from Luqman (the wise) to his son:

[31:13] (Remember) when Luqman said to his son, while he was advising him; My dear son, do not ascribe partners to Allah. Indeed, ascribing partners to Allah (shirk) is grave transgression.

[31:16] (Luqman went on saying to his son,) .My dear son, in fact, if there be anything to the measure of a grain of rye, and it be (hidden) in a rock or in the heavens or in the earth, Allah will bring it forth. Surely, Allah is All-Fine, All-Aware.

Investment for the future

Rewards of good parenting are not limited to the pride and joy felt knowing that parents have brought up a find young man or woman and contributing member of the society, but these rewards will continue to roll in even after the death of the parents.

Sayyidina Abu Huraira (RA) reported Allah's Messenger (Sallaho Alaihe Wassallam) as saying: When a man dies, his acts come to an end, but three, recurring charity, or knowledge (by which people) benefit, or a pious son, who prays for him (for the deceased). [Muslim]

Spending on Children (family) is charity!

Parents are encouraged to spend on their families and reminded of the immense reward of this expenditure in the hereafter. The noble Sunnah teaches us to be kind to our children and families to be spend on them to console them and make them feel happy.

Narrated Sayyidina Abu Masud Al-Badri (RA): The Prophet (Sallaho Alaihe Wassallam) said, "A man's spending on his family is a deed of charity." [Bukhari]

Fair and equal treatment of children:

Young children are sensitive and Islam teaches that the parents should be fair, equitable and just in treating their children. Human feelings are sometimes beyond ones' control but tangible actions should be well thought out and fair treatment of all children should be ensured.

Sayyidina 'Amir (RA) narrated: I heard An-Nu'man bin Bashir on the pulpit saying, "My father gave me a gift but 'Amra bint Rawaha (my mother) said that she would not agree to it unless he made Allah's Apostle as a witness to it. So, my father went to Allah's Apostle and said, 'I have given a gift to my son from 'Amra bint Rawaha, but she ordered me to make you as a witness to it, O Allah's Apostle!' Allah's Apostle asked, 'Have you given (the like of it) to everyone of your sons?' He replied in the negative. Allah's Apostle said, 'Be afraid of Allah, and be just to your children.' My father then returned and took back his gift." [Bukhari]

Nikah (Marriage) & Walima (Reception) in Islam

[24:32] Arrange the marriage of the spouseless among you, and the capable from among your bondmen and bondwomen. If they are poor, Allah will enrich them out of His grace. Allah is All-Encompassing, All-Knowing.

Importance of Marriage in Islam:

Islam has not only permitted Nikah but encouraged it and emphasised its importance. Muslim society has been commanded by Allah (SWT) to engage in Nikah and actively support each other in this endeavour:

[24:32] Arrange the marriage of the spouseless among you, and the capable from among your bondmen and bondwomen. If they are poor, Allah will enrich them out of His grace. Allah is All-Encompassing, All-Knowing.

Muslim women have also been discouraged to live a life of celibacy and commanded by Allah (SWT) to choose a suitable spouse:

[2:232] When you have divorced women, and they have reached (the end of) their waiting period, do not prevent them from marrying their husbands when they mutually agree with fairness. Thus the advice is given to everyone of you who believes in Allah and in the Hereafter. This is more pure and clean for you. Allah knows and you do not know.

In fact, Allah (SWT) describes his special blessings to Prophets (AS) having granted them wives and children:

[13:38] We have sent messengers before you, and gave them wives and children. It is not for a messenger to bring a verse without the will of Allah. For every age there are some rules prescribed.

Our beloved Rasul-ullah (Sallaho Alaihe Wassallam) also commanded Muslims to engage in Nikah as it is best for their character and modesty and helps them with guarding their gaze.

Narrated 'Abdullah (RA): We were with the Prophet (Sallaho Alaihe Wassallam) while we were young and had no wealth whatever. So Allah's Apostle (Sallaho Alaihe Wassallam) said, "O young people! Whoever among you can marry, should marry, because it helps him lower his gaze and guard his modesty (i.e. his private parts from committing illegal sexual intercourse etc.), and whoever is not able to marry, should fast, as fasting diminishes his sexual power." [Bukhari]

Warning to those who disregard marriage:

The Sunnah of Rasul-ullah (Sallaho Alaihe Wassallam) discourages from life of celibacy and abstinence from Nikah and equates abstinence from Nikah as not following the traditions of Islam.

Narrated Anas bin Malik (RA): A group of three men came to the houses of the wives of the Prophet asking how the Prophet worshipped (Allah), and when they were informed about that, they considered their worship insufficient and said, "Where are we from the Prophet as his past and future sins have been forgiven." Then one of them said, "I will offer the prayer throughout the night forever." The other said, "I will fast throughout the year and will not break my fast." The third said, "I will keep away from the women and will not marry forever." Allah's Apostle came to them and said, "Are you the same people who said so-and-so? By Allah, I am more submissive to Allah and more afraid of Him than you; yet I fast and break my fast, I do sleep and I also marry women. So he who does not follow my tradition in religion, is not from me (not one of my followers)." [Bukhari]

Legal Status of Marriage in Islam:

Shaykh (Mufti) Mohammed Sajjad writes, "Nikah is a very blessed Sunnah so much so that scholars have written to occupy oneself in arranging to marry, or in maintaining ones' marriage through earning a living etc. is preferred over performing extra (nafl) acts of worship, See Rad al-Muhtar, vol.4 p.57. Having said this, for a person who cannot control his gaze and is committing Zina of the eyes etc. it will be obligatory (wajib) to marry to preserve his Deen."

Shaykh (Maulana) Khalid Saifullah Rahmani writes in Halal wa Haram, "It is even recommended for a person who has sexual urges but doesn't fear that he will fall into Fitnah that he should marry and some have categorised his status (need) for Nikah as Sunnah while others as Mustahab (recommended) but in reality Nikah cannot be categorised as less then Sunnah and those who have declared it Mustahab (recommended) for him do actually mean that it is indeed Sunnah"

Procedure for Marriage in Islam:

Choosing a suitable partner:

Although beauty, physical attraction or a feature which is pleasing can be adopted as a means of choosing a partner as subtly hinted in the Qur'aan:

[4:3]...marry the women you like...

But the ultimate criteria and basis should be the religious inclination and practise of the individual.

Narrated Abu Huraira (RA): The Prophet (Sallaho Alaihe Wassallam) said, "A woman is married for four things, i.e., her wealth, her family status, her beauty and her religion. So you should marry the religious woman (otherwise) you will be a losers. [Bukhari]

A healthy marital life coupled with a good relationship make up the prime objects of Nikah. That is only possible when natural inclinations and backgrounds are shared (by both spouses). In the absence of such unity, living together successfully, despite great effort is indeed difficult, as attested to by many marital breakdowns due to non-compatibility.

Certain actions and situations elicit different responses from persons of differing backgrounds and nature. For this reason, the Shari'ah has considered Kafaa'at (suitability and compatibility) between spouses necessary.

Shaykh (Maulana) Khalid Saifullah Rahmani writes in Halal wa Haram, "Fuqaha have suggested nine (9) areas of Kafaa'at (suitability and compatibility) and they are:

Lineage

Being independent or enslaved

Born Muslim or being a Revert (to Islam)

Trustworthy and having Taqwa

Financial status

Honour and community standing

Profession & Trade

Free from physical defects

Intellect and Maturity

However, the main aspect for consideration is Deen & Akhlaq as Allamah Kasani (RA) has stated in Badai-us-sanai, "It is preferred by us to consider Deen and to rely on it exclusively" "

Looking at the potential partner:

Shaykh (Maulana) Khalid Saifullah Rahmani writes in Halal wa Haram, "Islamic Shariah wants the bonds of marriage to be strong and everlasting therefore it is recommended to look at the person beforehand and it is permitted to look at her in secret. However, looking should be with the intention of marrying and not for evil purposes and it is not permitted to spend time with the potential spouse in seclusion"

Narrated Jabir ibn Abdullah (RA): Rasul-ullah (Sallaho Alaihe Wassallam) said, "When one of you asked a woman in marriage, if he is able to look at what will induce him to marry her, he should do so. He (Jabir) said: I asked a girl in marriage, I used to look at her secretly, until I looked at what induced me to marry her. I, therefore, married her." [Abi Daud]

Venue for Marriage and publicising it:

Shaykh (Mufti) Ibraheem Desai writes, "It is Sunnah for the marriage to be pronounced and performed in the Masjid"

Aisha (RA) narrated that Rasul-ullah (Sallaho Alaihe Wassallam) said, "Publicise these marriages, conduct them in mosques, and beat the duff (tambourines) to announce them". [Tirmidhi]

Proposal & Acceptance, two male witnesses and Wakeel and the Dowry:

Since the purpose of Nikah is to safeguard a person's chastity and modesty, Islam has kept the procedure for Nikah very simple and straight forward.

Shaykh (Mufti) Ibraheem Desai writes, "Nikah is performed with a proposal (Iejaab) by the male or female and acceptance (Qubool) by the male or female in the past tense and in the presence of two male Muslim witnesses (Hidaaya vol. 2). The bride gives consent to her representative (Wakeel) in the presence of two witnesses to perform her marriage at the Masjid. At the Masjid, the Wakeel represents the bride in the presence of the two witnesses and the stipulated dowry. The witnesses must be two trustworthy and pious male Muslims who are not her ascendants e.g. father, grandfather or descendants e.g. son, grandson, etc. The Mahr (dowry) is the woman's right and should be stipulated prior to the marriage."

Aisha (RA) narrates that Rasul-ullah (Sallaho Alaihe Wassallam) said, "There is no marriage except with a wali and two witnesses of good character."[Bayhaqi]

Ibn Qudamah (RA) said: Marriage cannot be done except with two Muslim witnesses, whether the couple are both Muslims, or only the husband is Muslim...[Al-Mughni]

[4:4] Give women their dower in good cheer. Then, if they forego some of it, of their own will, you may have it as pleasant and joyful.

Forced marriage in Islam

All of the above is to be done with the permission and consent of the husband and wife. The case of forced marriages is discussed below.

Q) Five years ago I was coerced into a forced arranged marriage; I mumbled the words "accept" as I wanted to return back to the UK. Since that day I have had no contact with my "wife" and my family has realized that I am not happy. After 5 years they are ready to bring her over from Pakistan, however I do not feel that I can take her as my wife. I can't seem to see the qualities in her for a wife, and there are too many cultural differences, she is uneducated and I am a professional. I neither find her attractive and can't see any good characteristics - I wish for a practicing strong Muslim who will make my children good strong Muslims. I have tried to ask myself sincerely whether I could live with her as husband and wife, and if I can change her - but realistically I can't, and there is no

common ground. Though I am closer to my din than before, my family is non-practicing. Several discussions have occurred with my parents regarding this issue; all they believe is that it will work as they did the same. I intend to do istikharah. What do I do, and what is the ruling.

In the name of Allah, Most Compassionate, Most Merciful,

If you did accept her as your wife meaning that offer (ijab) and acceptance (qabul) did take place in the presence of two male witnesses, then you are considered Islamically married, hence she is your wife and you her husband. You state that you did say "accept", thus I presume your marriage is valid.

If you were forced into marrying her and you do not wish to remain married to her, then there would be nothing wrong Islamically in divorcing her. It is your right whom you marry, hence the decision is yours. At times, it is better to part ways in the early stages and before consummation, rather than have problems later on.

Thus, you need to really discuss matters with your parents, family, relatives and a local scholar of knowledge and piety. If you think you will not be able to maintain her as a wife and fulfill her rights, you may divorce her, as this would be lesser harm.

And Allah knows best

Muhammad ibn Adam al-Kawthari

Darul Iftaa, Leicester, UK

Q) 3 years ago I was forced married to my cousin in Pakistan against my will with threats to be killed etc. I have since then fought to get rid of that man, and now it seems that I will get my divorce soon InshaAllah. Since he is a cousin, the divorce will have some serious consequences for me. My parents have told me that they will not have any link with me if I get married again. Also I have been told that they - the male members of the family - will beat up the potential man if he is not from our clan (zaat, in urdu) [...] Now, after having described the situation, I would like to ask you whether it will be permissible for me to marry someone without the consent of my parents as they will never ever accept anyone that I will point on. I know for sure that I will try my best to convince them but they are not very cooperative as they

think that I have not cooperated with them on the cousin marriage.

In the name of Allah, Most Compassionate, Most Merciful,

You have a free choice and will to marry whosoever you want. Your parents cannot force you into marrying someone you don't want to marry. As such, when you are Islamically divorced, you may marry [after your waiting period (idda)] without the consent of your parents (due to the circumstances you have outlined in your question) as long as the potential spouse is considered a legal match (kuf').

And Allah knows best

Muhammad ibn Adam al-Kawthari

Darul   Iftaa,   Leicester,   UK

Minimum Dowry:

Shaykh (Mufti) Muhammad ibn Adam writes, "The least mehr which can be given is Ten dirhams (approximately 31 grams of silver). (Al Hidayaah). Today the mehr value is calculated by using the weight of silver which would equal the amount of dirhams. For example the mehr fatimi is 131.24 tolas. (this weight is constant is will not change). But the value of this amount of Silver is continuously changing according to the stock market. The change takes place every month or so. To be able to work out the approximate value for ten dirhams one can take the weight of the mehr Fatimi (131.25 tolas)and divide it by 400 (because 400 dirhams was the mehr which Hadhrat Fatimah was married with) and then multiply it by ten (to equal the weight of ten dirhams). This will give the value of silver which is equal to ten dirhams."

Shaykh (Maulana) Luqman Hansoot has detailed the minimum Meh'r and the Meh'r Fatimti (i.e. the dowry given to Sayyidituna Fatima (RA)) by Rasul-ullah (Sallaho Alaihe Wassallam) in the following table:

Type of Mehr	Dirhams (Silver)	Grams (Silver)	Troy Ounces (Silver)

Minimum	10	30.615175	0.9843
Meg'r Fatimi	480	1469.64495	47.24928

When Dowry was not stipulated?

Shaykh (Mufti) Muhammad ibn Adam writes, "If the dowry (mahr) was not stipulated in the contract of marriage, then the husband is obliged to pay what is "typically" received as marriage payment by similar brides (mahr al-mithl), if the marriage was consummated.

Imam al-Mawsili (Allah have mercy on him) states:

"If one did not fix dowry for her or one made a condition that she will not receive any dowry, she will receive what is typically received by similar brides (mahr al-mithl), if after consummation of marriage or death. She will receive a small gift (mut'a) in case of divorce before consummation." (al-Ikhtiyar li ta'lil al-Mukhtar, 2/126)"

Marriage Sermon (Khutbah):

Shaykh (Maulana) Khalid Saifullah Rahmani writes in Halal wa Haram, "The following is referred to us as 'Khutbatul-Hajjah" in Hadeeth and can be read at any occasion but in a narration of Baihaqi it has been linked with the occasion of Nikah"

إِنَّ الْحَمْدَ لِلَّهِ ، نَسْتَعِينُهُ وَنَسْتَغْفِرُهُ ، وَنَعُوذُ بِهِ مِن شُرُورِ أَنْفُسِنَا ، مَن يَهدِهِ اللَّهُ فَلا مُضِلَّ لَهُ ، وَمَن يُضلِلْ فَلا هَادِيَ لَهُ ، وَأَشهَدُ أَن لا إِلَهَ إِلا اللَّهُ وَأَشهَدُ أَنَّ مُحَمَّدًا عَبْدُهُ وَرَسُولُه .

يَا أَيُّهَا النَّاسُ اتَّقُواْ رَبَّكُمُ الَّذِي خَلَقَكُم مِّن نَّفْسٍ وَاحِدَةٍ وَخَلَقَ مِنْهَا زَوْجَهَا وَبَثَّ مِنْهُمَا رِجَالاً كَثِيراً وَنِسَاء وَاتَّقُواْ اللَّهَ الَّذِي تَسَاءلُونَ بِهِ وَالأَرْحَامَ إِنَّ اللَّهَ كَانَ عَلَيْكُمْ رَقِيباً

يَا أَيُّهَا الَّذِينَ آمَنُواْ اتَّقُواْ اللَّهَ حَقَّ تُقَاتِهِ وَلاَ تَمُوتُنَّ إِلاَّ وَأَنتُم مُّسْلِمُونَ

يَا أَيُّهَا الَّذِينَ آمَنُوا اتَّقُوا اللَّهَ وَقُولُوا قَوْلاً سَدِيداً يُصْلِحْ لَكُمْ أَعْمَالَكُمْ وَيَغْفِرْ لَكُمْ ذُنُوبَكُمْ وَمَن يُطِعْ اللَّهَ وَرَسُولَهُ فَقَدْ فَازَ فَوْزاً عَظِيماً

Praise be to Allaah, we seek His help and His forgiveness. We seek refuge with Allaah from the evil of our own souls and from our bad deeds. Whomsoever Allaah guides will never be led astray, and whomsoever Allaah leaves astray, no one can guide. I bear witness that there is no god but Allaah, and I bear witness that Muhammad (Sallaho Alaihe Wassallam) is His slave and Messenger

[4:1] O men, fear your Lord who created you from a single soul, and from it created its match, and spread many men and women from the two. Fear Allah in whose name you ask each other (for your rights), and fear (the violation of the rights of) the womb-relations. Surely, Allah is watchful over you.

[3:102] O you who believe, fear Allah, as He should be feared, and let not yourself die save as Muslims.

[33:70] O you who believe, fear Allah, and speak in straightforward words.[33:71] (If you do so,) Allah will correct your deeds for your benefit, and forgive your sins for you. Whoever obeys Allah and His Messenger achieves a great success.

Congratulating the Groom:

It is from the Sunnah of Rasul-ullah (Sallaho Alaihe Wassallam) to congratulate the groom with this dua:

بَارَكَ اللهُ لكَ وَبَارَكَ عَلَيْكَ وَجمَعَ بَيْنَكُمَا فِي الخَيْر

Sayyidina Abu Hurayrah (RA) reported that when a man married, Rasul-ullah (Sallaho Alaihe Wassallam) would say to him, "May Allah bless you and bless it for you and may He join you with goodness!" [Tirmidhi]

Feast of Walima:

Shaykh (Mufti) Muhammad ibn Adam writes, "The Arabic word Walima (marriage banquet) is derived from the root word Walam, which literally means to gather and assemble. The Arabs used it for a meal or feast where people were invited and gathered. Later, the term became exclusive for the wedding banquet. The Arabs used different terms for the various feasts they enjoyed. For example: al-I'zar on the occasion of a child's circumcision, al-Khurs for a marriage not ending in divorce, al-Wakira on building a new home, al-Naqi'ah when a traveller returns home, al-Aqiqah on the seventh day after childbirth, al-Ma'duba for a general meal without any specific reason, etc. (See: Ibn Hajar, Fath al-Bari, 9/300 & Ibn Qudamah, al-Mugni, 7/1). The marriage feast (walima) is a Sunna of our beloved Messenger of Allah (Allah bless him & give him peace). It is an outward expression of gratitude and pleasure and a great means of publicising the marriage, which has been greatly encouraged."

Sayyiduna Anas ibn Malik (RA) narrates that the Messenger of Allah (Sallaho Alaihe Wassallam) saw a yellow mark on Abdur Rahman ibn Awf (RA) and said: "What's this?" He replied: "I have married a woman with the dowry being gold to the weight of a date-stone." The Messenger of Allah (Sallaho Alaihe Wassallam) said: "May Allah bless you (in your marriage), perform a Walima, even if it is only with a goat." [Bukhari]

Shaykh (Maulana) Khalid Saifullah Rahmani writes in Halal wa Haram, "The Walima feast and its preparation is dependent upon the financial status and means of the individual as he (Sallaho Alaihe Wassallam) himself offered different varieties of feast on various occasions of his walima"

The Messenger of Allah (Sallaho Alaihe Wassallam) himself provided a Walima after many of his marriages. He provided meat and bread on the occasion of his marriage with Zaynab bint Jahsh (RA), Hays (a type of sweat-dish cooked with dates, cheese & butter) on the occasion of his marriage with Safiyya (RA) and barley on another occasion. [Bukhari & Muslim]

The time of Walima:

Shaykh (Mufti) Muhammad ibn Adam writes, "The scholars have disagreed as to the correct time of this Walima. There are many opinions. For example:

At the time of the marriage contract,

After the marriage contract and before consummation of marriage,

90

At the time of the wedding procession (bride leaving for her husband's house) (Ibn Hajar, Fath al-Bari, 9/287)

However, the majority of the scholars (jumhur) are of the opinion that Walima is a meal that is prepared after the marriage has been consummated. This was the practice of the Messenger of Allah (Allah bless him & give him peace), as explicitly mentioned in one narration.

Sayyiduna Anas ibn Malik (RA) narrates that he was a boy of ten when the Messenger of Allah (Sallaho Alaihe Wassallam) migrated to Madina. (He added): "My mother and aunts used to urge me to serve the Messenger of Allah (Sallaho Alaihe Wassallam) regularly, thus I served him for ten years. When the Messenger of Allah (Sallaho Alaihe Wassallam) passed away, I was twenty years old, and I knew about the order of Hijab more than anyone else, when it was revealed. It was revealed for the first time when the Messenger of Allah (Sallaho Alaihe Wassallam) had consummated his marriage with Zainab bint Jahsh (RA). The Messenger of Allah (Sallaho Alaihe Wassallam) in the morning was a bridegroom, and he invited the people to a banquet. So they came, ate, and then all left except a few who remained with the Messenger of Allah (Sallaho Alaihe Wassallam) for a long time..... [Bukhari]

Sayyiduna Anas (RA) said: "The Messenger of Allah (Sallaho Alaihe Wassallam) consummated his marriage with a woman (Zainab), so he sent me to invite people for a meal." [Bukhari]

The great Hadith master (hafidh), Ibn Hajar al-Asqalani (RA) states:

"The Hadith of Anas (quoted above) is clear in determining that Walima is considered to be after the consummation of marriage." (Fath al-Bari, 9/199. Also see: I'la al-Sunan, vol. 10, p. 11)

It is stated in al-Fatawa al-Hindiyya:

> "The marriage banquet (walima) is a Sunna and there is great reward in it. And it is carried out when the marriage is consummated." [al-Fatawa al-Hindiyya, 5/343]"

The Hanafi jurists (fuqaha) are of the opinion that, a banquet up to two days will be considered to be a Walima, after which it will no longer be considered a Walima.

It is stated in al-Fatawa al-Hindiyya:

> "There is nothing wrong in inviting people the next day after consummation or the day after. After that, marriage and Walima celebrations will come to an end." [5/343]

It has also been reported from the Messenger of Allah (Sallaho Alaihe Wassallam) that he stated:

> "Walima on the first day is confirmed (haq), and on the second day, it is good (ma'ruf), and on the third day, it is showing off." [Abi Daud]

Who should be invited to Walima?

Shaykh (Mufti) Muhammad ibn Adam writes, "Sayyiduna Abu Huraira (RA) states: "The worst food is that of a wedding banquet (walima) to which only the rich are invited whilst the poor are not invited. And he who refuses an invitation (to a banquet) disobeys Allah and His Messenger (Sallaho Alaihe Wassallam)." [Bukhari]

It is stated in al-Fatawa al-Hindiyya:

> "It is recommended to invite neighbours, relatives and friends." (5/343)

Thus, one should invite family-members, relatives, friends, associates, scholars and pious people and others. It is wrong to invite only rich people or those who are regarded to be from the upper-class.

The Islamic status of accepting the Walima invitation?

Shaykh (Mufti) Muhammad ibn Adam writes, "Sayyiduna Abd Allah ibn Umar (RA) narrates that the Messenger of Allah (Sallaho Alaihe Wassallam) said: "If one of you is invited to a wedding banquet (walima), then he must accept the invitation." [Bukhari]

Sayyiduna Abd Allah ibn Umar (RA) narrates that the Messenger of Allah (Sallaho Alaihe Wassallam): "Accept this (marriage) invitation if you are invited to it." And Abd Allah ibn Umar used to accept the invitation whether to a wedding banquet or to any other feast, even when he was fasting. [Bukhari]

Due to the above and other narrations, many scholars regard the acceptance of a Walima invitation to be binding, and one will be sinful for refusing it.

The great Hadith and Sahfi'i scholar, Imam al-Nawawi (RA) has mentioned various opinions of the scholars in this regard:

It is personally obligatory (fard ayn), except if there is an excuse,

It is a general obligation (fard kifaya)

It is recommended (mandub) (See: Nawawi, al-Minhaj, Sharh Sahih Muslim, 1080)

In the Hanafi Madhhab, the preferred opinion is that, accepting a Walima invitation is an emphatic Sunna (sunna al-Mu'akkada), and accepting other invitations is recommended (mandub). This is in normal cases, for if there is a valid reason, one will be excused from not attending.

Imam Ibn Abidin (Allah have mercy on him) states:

"The (hanafi) scholars have differed as to the ruling of accepting a Walima invitation. Some have stated that it is necessary (wajib), in that it is impermissible to refuse. However the majority of the scholars mention that it is a Sunna. It is better to accept it if it is a Walima invitation, otherwise (on other occasions) one has a choice to accept it, and to accept it would be better, because it creates joy and happiness in the heart of a Muslim.

When one accepts the invitation and attends the party, one has fulfilled the responsibility, regardless of whether one ate or otherwise, although it is better to eat if one is not fasting......It is stated in al-Ikhtiyar: "A Walima is an established Sunna. The one who does not accept it would be sinful, for the Messenger of Allah (Allah bless him& give him peace) said: "He who refuses an invitation (to a banquet) disobeys Allah and His Messenger (Allah bless him & give him peace)." If one is fasting, then one should attend and make Dua, and if not, then one should eat and make Dua. However, if one neither eats nor attends, then one will be sinful....

This indicates that accepting a Walima invitation is Sunna al-Mu'akkada, contrary to meals and invitations on other occasions. Some commentators of al-Hidaya have declared that it is close to being a Wajib." (Ibn Abidin, Radd al-Muhtar ala al-Durr, 6/349)

In light of Ibn Abidin's explanation, it becomes clear that accepting a Walima invitation is Sunna al-Mu'akkada, and one must accept it. Refusing to attend will be offensive if not sinful, provided one does not have an excuse, and also that one was specifically invited to the Walima."

Disagreeable customs, innovations and forbidden practises associated with Wedding:

Shaykh (Maulana) Saleem Dhorat writes, "In aping Western methods sheepishly, Muslims have adopted many customs which are un-Islamic and frowned upon. Some examples are:

Displaying the bride on stage;

Inviting guests for the wedding from far off places;

Receiving guests in the hall;

The bride's people incurring unnecessary expenses by holding a feast which has no basis in Shariah. We should remember that Walimah is the feast arranged by the bridegroom after the marriage is consummated.

It is contrary to Sunnah (and the practice of some non-Muslim tribes in India) to wish, hope for or demand presents and gifts for the bridegroom, from the bride's people. We should always remember that our Nabi (Sallaho Alaihe Wassallam) did not give Ali (RA) anything except Dua"

Shaykh (Maulana) Saleem Dhorat previously narrates the blessed wedding of Siyyidituna Fatima and Sayydina Ali (RA) and concludes that the following methods can be derived from it:

The many customs as regards engagement are contrary to the Sunnah. In fact, many are against the Shariah and are regarded as sins. A verbal proposal and answer is sufficient.

To unnecessarily delay Nikah of both the boy and the girl after having reached the age of marriage is incorrect.

There is nothing wrong in inviting one's close associates for the occasion of Nikah. However, no special pains should be taken in gathering the people from far off places.

It is appropriate that the bridegroom be a few years older than the bride.

If the father of the girl is a Scholar or pious and capable of performing Nikah, then he should himself solemnise the marriage.

It is better to give the Mahr Faatimi and one should endeavour to do so. But if one does not have the means then there is nothing wrong in giving less.

It is totally un-Islamic for those, who do not possess the means, to incur debts in order to have grandiose weddings.

It is fallacy to think that one's respect will be lost if one does not hold an extravagant wedding and invite many people. What is our respect compared to that of (Sallaho Alaihe Wassallam)?

The present day practice of the intermingling of sexes is an act of sin and totally against Shariah.

There is nothing such as engagement parties and Medhi parties in Islam.

Great care must be taken as regards to Salaat on occasions of marriage by all - the bride, the bridegroom and all the participants.

It is un-Islamic to display the bride on stage.

The unnecessary expenses incurred by the bride's family in holding a feast has no basis in Shariah.

For the engaged couple to meet at a public gathering where the boy holds the girl's hand and slips a ring on her finger is a violation of the Qur'anic law of Hijaab.

It is un-Islamic for the engaged couple to meet each other and also go out together.

Three things should be borne in mind when giving one's daughter gifts and presents at the time of Nikah:

Presents should be given within one's means (it is not permissible to take loans, on interest for such presents);

To give necessary items;

A show should not be made of whatever is given.

It is Sunnat for the bridegroom's family to make Walimah. In Walimah, whatever is easily available should be fed to the people and care should be taken that the is no extravagance, show and that no debts are incurred in the process.

To delay Nikah after the engagement is un-Islamic.

Confused: My Marriages Failed Despite Istikhara

Q.) I am extremly perplexed and grieved concerning my present situation and shaytan is also attacking me with various iman endangering thoughts. Please can you answer my following question and put my mind at rest. I married a woman about 3 years ago. I went to see her and everything was done the Islamic way. i.e. I did Mashwera (consultation) and Istikhara (and I saw good dreams and my heart felt content.) But despite the istikhara, etc. Our marriage broke up after just a few weeks of living together, as it transpired that she was mentally unstable.

I married again this year, this time I was extra cautious and therefore did Istikhara over a long period and begged Allah to guide me, as a result of which I saw many good dreams. I also had the dreams interpreted by a scholar who gave me the go ahead. After that I did consultation with my superiors and they also gave me the go ahead. But, Again this marriage has broken down in a short span of time.

Why is it that both my marriages have failed (through no fault of mine, I tried my best both times) even though I did Istikhara and Mashwera both times and felt content at heart.

Please reply soon and put my mind at rest, I am losing hope and shaytan is playing with my mind and making me doubt the words of Allah and his Prophet. (naoozobillah) Please reply soon. Jazakallah. A distressed brother in need. [s.m.]

A.) Istikhara is a particular form of prayer and the masnoon way of doing is that a person offers 2 Rakats with the intention of Istikhara then recites the Dua for Istikhara which may be found in all the books of prayer. The other ways of Istikhara which are suggested by some persons are not masnoon. So far as the effect of Istikhara is concerned you must observe the following points:

First of all you must know that Istikhara is nothing more than a normal Dua in which a person prays to Allah Subhanahu Taala to guide him to reach a right decision. It is not correct to presume that in response to an Istikhara Allah gives an answer in the form of a dream. Similarly it is not necessary that a dream is seen after making an Istikhara and even though a dream is seen by the relevant person it is not an absolute answer towards a particular direction because dream is not treated in Shariah as a binding proof of something. The expected result of Istikhara is that the relevant person himself takes a decision which is good for him in this world or in the hereinafter or in both. But just as the grant of other prayers depends on certain conditions the Istikhara is subject to those conditions as well. If some of these conditions are lacking, it is not necessary that this prayer is granted

Second, to make an Istikhara does not mean that a person abandons all other necessary enquiries. A person must carry out all efforts necessary to reach a correct decision even after making Istikhara. If a person is content on Istikhara only and does not make the required efforts to reach the correct decision he may fall into error.

Third, in this particular case the reason for breakup of marriages is not certainly known. It is possible that the marriage failed not because the decision to marry that woman was wrong but because the husband could not properly handle the marriage. In other words it is possible that the decision to marry the woman was correct but the decision to divorce her was wrong.

Fourth, as mentioned in the first point in some rare cases Istikhara does not prove to be fruitful in this world but it is certain to be fruitful in the world hereinafter.

Fornication, Adultery, Masturbation, Pornography, Oral & Anal Sex

Sayyidina Abdullah Ibn Mas'ud (RA) reported that Allah's Messenger (may peace be upon him) said to us: O young men, those among you who can support a wife should marry, for it restrains eyes (from casting evil glances) and preserves one from immorality; but he who cannot afford It should observe fast for it is a means of controlling the sexual desire. [Muslim].

Is it wrong to Learn about Matters that are of a Sexual Nature?

By Shaykh (Mufti) Muhammad Ibn Adam (HA)

Question: Recently, a course was advertised in our city teaching aspects of sexual intimacy between married couples. Some people in our community objected saying that such a course goes against Adab and modesty. Are there any grounds for this ?

Answer: In the Name of Allah, Most Compassionate, Most Merciful,

Islam is a complete way of life that provides guidance in every aspect of a believer's life, from purity and prayer, to trade regulations, marriage and inheritance laws. There is little place for the separation of religion from the state, rather, Islam insists on adherence to the full spectrum of its teachings – from the fundamental articles of faith (aqa'id) and devotional worship (ibadaat), to financial transactions (mu'amalaat), social and communal etiquettes (mu'ashara) and moral ethics (akhlaq). Allah Most High says:

"O you who believe, enter into Islam completely, and do not follow the footsteps of Satan. Surely he is an open enemy for you." (Qur'an 2:208)

The Messenger of Allah (Allah bless him & give him peace), being an exemplar of perfection, showed us the way to that which is of benefit in both worlds, even in the mundane realities of everyday life.

Imam Muslim (Allah have mercy on him) relates in his Sahih from the Companion Salman al-Farisi (Allah be pleased with him) that some polytheists approached him saying,"Your Prophet has taught you everything, even about excrement [i.e. etiquettes of relieving oneself]." He replied: "Indeed! He has forbidden us from facing the Qibla when excreting or urinating, and from cleaning ourselves with our right hand, and from cleaning ourselves with less than three stones, and from cleaning ourselves with dung or bone." (Sahih Muslim 262 & Sunan Abi Dawud 7)

Sayyiduna Abu Hurayra (Allah be pleased with him) relates that the Messenger of Allah (Allah bless him & give him peace) said:"Verily, I am to you like a father, I teach you [i.e. do not be ashamed in learning even the basics from me]. If any one of you goes to relieve himself, he must not face the Qibla nor turn his back toward it, and must not clean himself with his right hand..." (Sunan Abi Dawud 8)

Similarly, Islam does not neglect one of the most private moments in an individual's life - namely, the sexual relationship between a husband and wife. Detailed and explicit rulings regarding sexual behaviour can be found in the Qur'an, Sunna and works of classical scholars. It is common to find scholars dedicating whole chapters in their works to this delicate, yet important, subject. Imam Abu Hamid al-Ghazali's Ihya Uloom al-Din, Al-Tibb al-Nabawi by Imam Ibn al-Qayyim al-Jawziyya, Imam Ibn Qudama's Al-Mughni, Imam Nasa'i's Ishrat al-Nisa', Imam Abu 'l-Faraj Ibn al-Jawzi's Sayd al-Khatir, the Ghunyat al-Talibin by Shaykh Abdul Qadir al-Jilani and countless other classical works deal with this topic in some detail. The major reference works in all four Sunni Schools of Islamic law (madhhabs) also discuss many aspects of sexual relations and what married couples may and may not do.

The reason for this is that a healthy sexual relationship is absolutely vital in marriage. Scholars today generally agree that one of the primary reasons for failed marriages is failed sexual lives. The root cause of marital discord is often sexual dissatisfaction, with problems in the bedroom often leading to unhappiness, frustration, and, at times, even divorce. Among the objectives of marriage is to satisfy one's sexual needs in a lawful manner, and if either spouse is unfulfilled, the temptation to look elsewhere can become overwhelming. Often, a spouse will refuse to engage in a form of sexual activity, mistakenly believing it to be unlawful, which could easily sour their relationship. It is therefore of key importance for married couples to learn and understand the teachings of Islam regarding sexual behaviour.

Moreover, in the modern world, there is a kind of fixation with sexuality. The topic has been institutionalised in the school curriculum under the banner of "sex education", where children are taught what some may consider shameful and sordid acts. The increasing pervasiveness of sexual imagery is affecting Muslims, with growing numbers becoming addicted to pornography and other unlawful means of sexual gratification.

In this environment, it is not only permitted but crucial to present the Islamic stance on this subject; otherwise Muslims will be left to learn about it from un-Islamic resources, damaging their character, spirituality and physical health.

Unfortunately, some Muslims consider any discussion on sex to be offensive and a breach of religious propriety (adab) and modesty (haya), unaware that the Messenger of Allah (Allah bless him & give him peace) himself explained this subject in considerable detail. Several hadiths describe how the Messenger of Allah (Allah bless him & give him peace) taught men and women matters relating to sexual relations.

Imam Bukhari and Imam Muslim (Allah have mercy on them) both record a hadith in their Sahih collections, related by Abu Hurayra (Allah be pleased with him), in which the Messenger of Allah (Allah bless him & give him peace) was teaching his Companions the rules of having a ritual bath (ghusl), when he said: "When a man sits amidst her four parts and then exerts pressure on her, a ritual bath becomes obligatory upon him." (Sahih al-Bukhari 287 & Sahih Muslim 348)

In this hadith, the Messenger of Allah (Allah bless him & give him peace) describes explicitly how a man might have sex with his wife such that it necessitates a ritual bath of purification. There are numerous other examples which illustrate the frankness with which the Messenger of Allah (Allah bless him & give him peace) discussed these matters.

The Companions (Allah be pleased with them) also did not shy away from asking the Messenger of Allah (Allah bless him & give him peace) questions of a sexual nature. In a famous incident, Sayyiduna Umar ibn al-Khattab (Allah be pleased with him) asked the Messenger of Allah (Allah bless him & give him peace) about the permissibility of penetrating one's wife from behind, i.e. penetrating the vagina, and not the anus. The Messenger of Allah (Allah bless him & give him peace) did not rebuke him for asking an "offensive" question, but waited until Allah Most High Himself revealed verses of the Qur'an to answer his question. (See: Sunan al-Tirmidhi 2980)

Remarkably, women also felt able to ask the Messenger of Allah (Allah bless him & give him peace) questions of a sexual nature without any reluctance or being ashamed of such enquiry. Rather, the Messenger of Allah (Allah bless him & give him peace) did not shy away from answering them, even though he was shy by nature.

Umm Salama (Allah be pleased with her) relates that Umm Sulaym (Allah be pleased with her) came to the Messenger of Allah (Allah bless him & give him peace) and said, "O Messenger of Allah, Surely, Allah is not shy of the truth. Is it necessary for a woman to take a ritual bath after she has a wet dream?" The Messenger of Allah (Allah bless him & give him peace) replied: "Yes, if she notices a discharge." Umm Salama covered her face and asked, "O Messenger of Allah! Does a woman have a discharge?" He replied: "Yes, let your right hand be in dust [an Arabic expression said light-heartedly to someone whose statement you contradict], how does the son resemble his mother?" (Sahih al-Bukhari 130)

Here, a woman has no qualms in asking the Messenger of Allah (Allah bless him & give him peace) about something as intimate as a wet dream. Umm Sulaym's statement, "Allah is not shy of the truth" is a clear indication that there is no shyness when it comes to learning about matters of Deen. The Messenger of Allah (Allah bless him & give him peace) used this phrase himself when he prohibited anal sex, saying:

"Allah is not shy of the truth; do not enter women in their anuses." (Sunan Ibn Majah 1924, Musnad Ahmad & others)

It is clear from the above that there is nothing wrong in discussing this subject for instructional purposes, as long as it is done with decency. In fact, it is a mistake to shy away from the teachings of Allah Most High and the Messenger (Allah bless him & give him peace), even those regarding sexual matters.

Imam Bukhari relates from Mujahid who said: "Sacred knowledge (ilm) is not gained by a shy person or an arrogant one (Sahih al-Bukhari 1:60)

Likewise, he relates from Sayyida A'isha (Allah be pleased with her) who said: "How praiseworthy are the women of Ansar; shyness does not prevent them from having a deep understanding of religion." (Ibid)

Those who feel uncomfortable with this subject should keep in mind the words of Allah Most High, His Messenger (Allah bless him & give him peace) and the Companions: "Surely, Allah is not shy of [expounding] the truth" (Qur'an 33:53, Sahih al-Bukhari 130 and Sunan Ibn Majah 1924).

Modesty is, without doubt, a fundamental element of our religion, but when it comes to religious matters it should not prevent one from learning, but rather, modesty should be exhibited when learning about such matters. In the modern world, questions of sexuality are openly discussed, often indecently; why then should we, as Muslims, feel ashamed of learning the pure and decent teachings of Islam on this subject?

In conclusion, there is nothing wrong with teaching, studying and learning the rules of Shari'ah regarding sexual relations with one's spouse. However, one should be careful not to violate the spirit of Islam of modesty, decency and bashfulness. Proper care should be taken of the language used and examples given. It would be wise that male students are taught by a male teacher, and female students by a female teacher. If these matters are taken care off, not only will this be allowed, it would fulfil a great need of the time, Insha Allah.

And Allah Knows Best

[Mufti] Muhammad ibn Adam

Darul Iftaa

Leicester , UK

Haraam Fantasizing

By Shaykh (Maulana) Yunus Patel (RA)

There is no shortage of complaints when it comes to giving up sins and the struggle which ensues between individuals and their nafs, as well as Shaytaan.

This battle is inevitably on-going – till our dying day. There is no other way out, except to show the courage and bravery that every Muslim does have – when it comes to Pleasing Allah Ta'ala.

Yet another widespread weakness is that of Haraam fantasizing. Young and old, married and unmarried – thousands upon thousands, succumb to their runaway imagination when it comes to fantasy world and this in turn leads to even graver sin.

Allah Ta'ala granted us the power of Imagination for a beautiful purpose; but most people today utilize this imagination in filthy thoughts. The following is actually drawn from my Malfoozaat. It is an extract from one of the kitaabs. It is a prescription which I have given to many who have complained of the same. Alhamdulillah, it has been a means of cure for many. May Allah Ta'ala make it a means of cure for all that have this ailment.

"Haraam fantasizing is the spiritual disease of almost every person. It is abuse of the great, wonderful and amazing gift of imagination.

Why did Allah Ta'ala give us this gift of imagination ?

The imagination has been given to us so that it may be used to ponder over the Qur`aan Sharif, which entails stories of past nations and verses upon verses of Jannat and Jahannum and accountability. This is imagination was to be used for the purpose of taking lesson and strengthening our Imaan. It was to be used as a catalyst towards 'Aml' (action).

106

The imagination was not given to us so that we may indulge our nafs in filthy thoughts.

One of the main reasons why both men and women have this problem plaguing them, is due to their indulgence in lustful gazing.

After having cast filthy gazes at ghair-mahareem , or watching porn movies or paging through porn magazines, or reading explicit romance novels, there is desire and craving for more. Since 'more' is generally not possible ... since the person may be married, or the object of one's desire is a film star or supermodel or a Miss Universe or Mr. Universe, and there is zero chance of meeting the person, the person tries to satisfy these shahawaat (desires) by fantasizing.

But fantasizing is not going to satisfy desire. It will only increase desire. The person's sickness will increase. His physical health will inevitably also suffer.

When the desire to indulge in Haraam fantasizing comes into the heart, then take your imagination to the Day of Judgement; stand before Allah Ta'ala's Seat of Judgement and begin accounting for all your actions in this world. Think of how you will account for and what you will say to Allah Ta'ala when all these filthy thoughts will be presented to you.

Allah Ta'ala states in the Qur`aan Sharif :

"WHEN THE SCROLLS ARE LAID OPEN." [SURAH TAKWEER 81 :10]

"THIS OUR RECORD SPEAKS ABOUT YOU WITH TRUTH : FOR WE WERE WONT TO PUT ON RECORD ALL THAT YOU DID." [SURAH JATHIYA 45 :29]

Even though Allah Ta'ala is All-Knowing and well aware of all our actions, He has established a law whereby every action and every detail of every action be recorded and thereafter presented to us

107

on the Day of Reckoning – in favour of us or witness against us.

Otherwise take your imagination for Haj : Picture yourself at the Multazam, making Tawaaf, making Sa`ee; picture yourself at the Raudha Mubarak, conveying Salaam to Rasulullah (sallallahu alayhi wasallam), or take your imagination to your Qabr and the events which unfold in the grave after death. ...Insha-Allah, this will a means of defeating nafs and Shaytaan as well as obliterating a filthy habit.

If you find yourself still weak against the demands of nafs and whisperings of Shaytaan, then immediately occupy yourself in that which is 'mubaah' (permissible). Begin conversation with your parents, or with brothers and sisters, or phone a good, pious friend, or listen to some Qiraat or Deeni talk... Occupy yourself in that which is Halaal and mubaah; otherwise nafs will ravage your heart and destroy your peace of mind and lead you to even suicidal tendencies.

Added to this, consider filthy thoughts as pigs. Just as we show aversion and absolute disgust on seeing a pig, so should we be disgusted with dirty thoughts – which fall in the same category as pigs. Both are Haraam (forbidden).

Furthermore, Haraam fantasizing leads to the evil habit of self-gratification, because there is no Halaal avenue to satisfy one's desires. This is a rather disastrous weakness amongst the youth and one should ponder over the various harms which are too many, and these harms are spiritual, physical and psychological harms.

Satisfying one's desires by masturbating is not permissible even if a person does not have the means to marry. Allah Ta'ala mentions that those who do not find the means to marry should remain chaste.

"And those who do not find the means to marry, should remain chaste until Allah gives them resources by His Grace

Remaining chaste is thus a Divine command which is compulsory to comply with – therefore we will find the Ahadith presenting prescriptions to remain chaste (lowering the gaze, fasting, etc.).

As a prescription, the following harms should be read and re-read if need be, until it is understood that the harms long term are not worth the gratification that comes with the sin.

Some Spiritual Harms :

Taufeeq of doing good deeds is taken away. The person is deprived of Tahajjud, of Tilawat of the Qur`aan Sharief, of associating with the pious, etc.

The person is deprived of knowledge and finds an aversion to people

The most dangerous is that the person will not be able to remain steadfast on Deen. (Allah Ta'ala protect).

Besides this, a person who satisfies his evil desires in this manner is cursed according to Rasulullah (sallallahu alayhi wasallam).

Some Physical harms :

The following physical harms have been recorded by highly qualified Hakims, the equivalent of specialist doctors.

The bladder becomes weak and this leads to problems in respect to taharah – Wudhu/ salaah and other Ibaadah. There are many that are suffering with involuntary urinary and seminal discharges due to the indulgence in this sin, and they write mentioning the difficulties that are thereafter encountered.

It also weakens the nerves.

It causes some limbs like the legs to shake and shiver.

It causes pain in the vertebra column, the spinal column from which semen is ejaculated. This pain creates crookedness and twisting in the back.

It creates weakness in the brain and weakness of memory.

It weakens the sight and reduces the normal limit of vision.

It causes a person to become old before time.

It decreases the natural resistence of the body.

It causes harm to the four principle organs in the body : the heart, brain, liver and stomach.

It weakens the fine nerves and veins of the sexual organs, resulting in impotency.

Excessive loss of semen is in reality excessive loss of blood. In later years, it can be that such a person will not have the ability to father any children.

It causes an excessive loss of sperm by way of nocturnal emission (wet dreams).

Some Psychological Harms :

It leads to:

agitation and irritation over trivial matters,

lack of confidence,

disinterest in studying

and desire for isolation.

Much more can be stated in respect to the harms of this sin. So contemplating the above, should give every incentive to give up the sin. No one would like to contend with any one of the above problems and yet just one evil deed and the person has invited waves of calamities upon himself.

If evil desires still get the better, then Nikah is a simple solution. Where the evil desires are so difficult to suppress that the person engages in Haraam then Shariah says that it is Fardh for the person to marry. This is, of course, for those who the ability.

Nikaah, Zina, Fornication: it is overlooked by Allah?

By Shaykh (Mufti) Muhammad Ibn Adam (HA)

Question: I have a cousin who has intentions of having his Nikkah done, to help prevent him form the sins of kissing, touching etc. He has all intentions of Eventually getting married to this sister. The parents on both sides are not agreeing to have it done. He was going to do it secretly, but now he has found something he believes is a way out?

Answer: In the Name of Allah, Most Compassionate, Most Merciful,

Let us first look at the translation of the verse towards which you have referred. Allah Most High says in Surah al-Najm:

> To Allah belongs all that is in the heavens and on earth, so that He rewards those who do evil, according to their deeds, and He rewards those who do good, with what is best. Those who avoid great sins and shameful deeds, only (falling into) small faults (lamam), verily your Lord is ample in forgiveness (53: 31-32).

Allah Almighty mentions in the first verse that those who do good and follow His guidance will be rewarded, and in the second verse, He describes such people by stating: Those who avoid great sins and shameful deeds, only falling into small faults, meaning falling into small faults does not exempt them from the address of the first verse.

The commentators of the Qur'an (mufassirun) generally mention two views from the companions and their followers (Allah be pleased with them all) with regards to the interpretation on the word "lamam".

112

It refers to minor sins that may be forgiven with many different acts of worship and good deeds, as mentioned in another verse:

If you refrain from the most heinous of the things which you are forbidden to do, we shall forgive your (minor) faults, and admit you to a gate of great honour (al-Nisa, 31).

Then, the majority of the scholars agree on the fact that persistence on minor sins amounts to a major sin, thus one must also try his best to refrain from minor sins.

Lamam means to accidentally and inadvertently commit a sin, whether major or minor, instantly repent from the sin and never to commit it again. This has also been mentioned in another verse, Allah Most High says:

And those who, having committed a major sin, or wronged their own souls, earnestly bring Allah to mind, and ask for forgiveness for their sins-and who can forgive sins except Allah- and are never obstinate in persisting knowingly in (the wrong) they have done. For such the reward is forgiveness from their lord, and gardens with rivers flowing underneath (Surah Ali Imran, 135-136).

Therefore, the meaning of the verses of Surah al-Najm is either to commit minor sins (infrequently) or commit a major sin accidentally, and then to abstain from it instantly and repent from Allah Almighty. Such people will not be exempted from the rewards Allah has promised for those who are considered good-doers (muhsinun). (See: Tafsir Ibn Kathir, 4/327-328 & Ma'arif al-Qur'an, 8/211-212).

As for fornication and whatever leads to it, such as touching, kissing, embracing, informal interaction are all considered to be major sins. Allah Most High states:

> Do not come (even) near to adultery, for it is a shameful (deed) and an evil, opening the road to other evils (Surah al-Isra, 32).

Thus, any form of fornication is totally unlawful (haram) in Islam, and to say that it is only a minor sin is incorrect.

As mentioned previously, the only meaning of the verse of Surah al-Najm is that one is absolutely resolute on refraining from these sins but they accidentally occurred, and repentance is made at once. After this, it is hoped from the mercy of Allah that such a person will remain considered one of those do good (muhsinun).

However, the verse does not in any way mean that one may be casual about these things, and regard them to be minor sins, for that is a great error.

The brother should at once stop any informal interaction with the sister. If they fear falling into the unlawful, then they must talk to their parents about getting married. If the parents do not agree, then they should use the intermediary of someone their parents respect such as a religious scholar, to explain to them, and if all avenues fail, then they may get married, but for that they must consult a reliable scholar and discuss the matter with him.

And Allah Knows Best

[Mufti] Muhammad ibn Adam

Darul Iftaa

Leicester , UK

Is it Permissible to have Phone Sex with One's Wife?

By Shaykh (Mufti) Muhammad Ibn Adam (HA)

Question: Is it permissible to have phone sex with one's wife?

Answer: In the Name of Allah, Most Compassionate, Most Merciful,

Phone sex refers to sexual conversations between two persons over the telephone. It is defined as a telephone conversation between two people whose objective is to arouse, titillate and stimulate one another. The point of phone sex is to help the partner in achieving orgasm through masturbation. "Phone sex" is frequently put in quotation marks because sex is usually associated with at least touching each other.
Phone sex is very similar to cyber sex, although the latter is typically free of charge. Cyber sex is the logical continuation of phone sex on modern computer networks. It is often seen as a simulation of "real" sex, and participants usually try to make the experience as close to real life as possible. It can be considered a form of role playing that allows a couple to experience sexual sensations without actually physically being in each other's company. (Webster's online dictionary)

As far as the Islamic ruling on phone and cyber sex is concerned, obviously engaging in them with someone to whom one is not legally married is completely and decisively unlawful (haram). Intimate conversations with other than one's spouse is without doubt immoral, sinful, blameworthy and unlawful, especially calling commercial sex phone lines and destroying one's morals, ethics and wealth.

As far as legally married couples being involved in phone sex is concerned, there are two situations here:

If the objective is to arouse one's spouse and guide him/her in masturbation to the point of having an orgasm, then this would not be allowed. Masturbation is sinful, being prohibitively disliked, and having many personal and societal ill-effects that are known and recognised in sane traditional societies and by balanced people the world over. However, mutual masturbation between the spouses is permitted. (Ibn Abidin, Radd al-Muhtar, 2/400)

During the course of a phone conversation, it will not be permitted for either of the spouses to masturbate. It cannot be called mutual masturbation, as that is when one satisfies one's self with a part of one's spouse's body. Thus, it will not be permitted for one to fantasize and play with oneself to the point of having an orgasm.

If during a phone conversation, the objective is not to masturbate; rather the spouses are merely intimate, then this would be permitted. It would be permitted to have an erotic and sexual conversation with one's spouse, provided one does not fear falling into masturbation or any other unlawful act.

It is completely lawful to think of one's spouse in a sexual way, hence there seems no hindrance from fantasizing about one's husband or wife.

If one avoids masturbation, but has an orgasm by merely having an erotic conversation with one's spouse, then this also does not seem to fall into the unlawful, provided the objective was not to masturbate or have an orgasm.

Finally, if there is no need for this, meaning if the couple are not distant from one another, it would be best to avoid it, as it is also a form of wasteful expenditure. However, couples who are distant from one another may be intimate over the phone or internet.

And Allah Knows Best

[Mufti] Muhammad ibn Adam

Darul Iftaa Leicester , UK

Employing Sex Toys During Intercourse

By Shaykh (Mufti) Muhammad Ibn Adam (HA)

Question: Is it permissible to use an external (clitoral) vibrator on one's wife during intercourse?

Answer: In the Name of Allah, Most Compassionate, Most Merciful,

Sexual relations between the spouses are vital and one of the most important aspects of marriage. It purifies and prevents one from falling into fornication and the unlawful. As such, the spouses may fulfil their sexual needs in any way they desire as long as it does not violate any injunction of Shariah.

Islam also generally abstained from placing too many restrictions with regards to bedroom behaviour; rather (with the exception of certain harmful and unhealthy practices) it left it to the spouses as how they should enjoy one another in their sexual relations.

From the various forms of pleasing one another, the usage of sex toys/aides, such as vibrators, dildos, lubricants, etc has become (or is becoming) a common phenomenon. Islamically, there is nothing wrong in using such toys provided the following conditions are met:

The toy must not be harmful in any way to the spouses, for inflicting harm upon your self is unlawful,

The toy must not have an animate figure to it,

It should not be inserted into the inner-private part of the women; rather only such toys should be used that stimulate the outer private parts, such as the clitoris.

If the above conditions are taken care of, coupled with the permission and consent of the spouse, then there seems no hindrance from employing such toys.

Having said that, it must be remembered that, it is unlawful to use such toys alone to alleviate one's loneliness, etc, for this would be considered a form of masturbation, which is unlawful (haram) and sinful.

Therefore, if there is a fear that by using these aides/toys during intercourse with one's spouse, one may be tempted to employ them when alone, then they must be avoided altogether.

And Allah Knows Best

[Mufti] Muhammad ibn Adam

Darul Iftaa

Leicester , UK

The Issue of Oral Sex

By Shaykh (Mufti) Muhammad Ibn Adam (HA)

Question: I would like to ask a question which people have either shied away or have been afraid to discuss. I tried to look in some Islamic books but there is no clear guidance that   I   could   find.

There are many married couples who are not sure about this but have not had the courage to ask including myself up until now. I would like to know what the Islamic shariah ruling is on the subject of sex between husband and wife. Is it permissible for the husband and wife to take or touch each others private parts in each others mouth?

I do hope that you will help with this.

Answer: In the Name of Allah, Most Compassionate, Most Merciful,

Firstly, it should be understood that Islam is a religion of modesty and shame. It encourages its followers to be modest and not have the instincts of animals. Modesty is one of the things which distinguish a human being from an animal.

However, this should not prevent one from learning about matters relating to sexual behaviour. Then Sahaba (Allah be pleased with them) were never shy and ashamed in learning the truth. There are many incidents where the companions came to the Messenger of Allah (Allah bless him and give him peace) and inquired about matters relating to sex. Even the Prophet (Allah bless him & give him peace), despite being very modest and bashful by nature, did not feel ashamed to discuss matters regarding the do's and don'ts of   sexual   relations.

To   proceed   with   the   answer   to   your   question:

119

The issue of oral sex is frequently asked. Many people shy away from it, whilst others regard discussing it offensive. However, those people who live in the "real" world will know the importance of mentioning this topic. Therefore, it is important to mention the Islamic perspective on oral sex in detail.

There are certain acts which have been clearly prohibited in Shariah, that are:

Anal sex

Anal sex is strictly prohibited in Islam. There are many narrations of the Messenger of Allah (Allah bless him and give him peace) which emphasize this.

In a Hadith recorded by Imam an-Nasa'i and others, the Messenger of Allah (Allah bless him & give him peace) said:

"Allah will not look (with mercy) at the one that has anal sex with his wife" (meaning on the day of Qiyamah). (Sunan Nasa'i

Sex during menstruation (Haidh)

The Qur'an has clearly and explicitly prohibited sexual intercourse during menstruation. Allah Most High says:

"They ask you (O Prophet) regarding menstruation. Say: It his hurtful and impure. So abstain from women (sexually) in menstruation." (Sura al-Baqarah, V.222)

The above two things are clearly prohibited by the Qur'an and Sunnah. When books of Fiqh talk about what is lawful and what is not, they typically mention that a husband and wife may give pleasure to one another in any way they wish other than the above mentioned things.

Although not specific to sex, we can add the following:

Swallowing filth (sexual fluids of the wife or husband)

Needlessly getting filthy

These things are obvious as sexual fluids and filth is impure.

There are also certain acts which are disliked, but permissible, for example: Total nudity, excessive sexual intercourse, etc...

Oral sex

As far as oral sex is concerned, there are two aspects to the issue. One being the moral aspect and the other the actual ruling regarding it in Islamic Law (meaning, to state whether it is Haram, Makruh or permissible).

With regards to the first aspect, there is no doubt that the act of oral sex (in its full meaning) is a totally shameful act. The mouth which is used to recite the Dhikr of Allah, send Salutations on the blessed Messenger of Allah (Allah bless him and give him peace), recite the holy Qur'an and other things, can not be used for filthy and dirty things such as oral sex, especially if it includes the filth entering the mouth.

This is more or less what the scholars of the Indo/Pak mention in there Fatawa books and (according to this humble servant), this is the aspect (moral) they are referring to.

As far as the second aspect is concerned, which is the Shariah ruling on oral sex; this actually depends on what you really mean by oral sex. The term "oral sex" covers a wide range of activities, from just kissing the private parts to the actual swallowing of filth.

If "oral sex" means to insert the penis in the wife's mouth to the extent that she takes in the filth, whether this filth is semen (Mani) or pre-ejaculatory fluid (Madhi), or the man takes the filth of the woman in his mouth, then this is not permissible. Taking the filth with all its forms in the mouth is unlawful. The fluids which come out are impure, thus make it impermissible to take it orally.

However, if the same act is practiced by using a condom (to prevent the sexual fluids entering the mouth) or the wife merely kisses her husband's penis and the husband kisses her genitals and they avoid any areas where there is pre-ejaculatory fluid, then this should be (according to this humble servant and Allah knows best) permissible, although disliked.

It is mentioned in the famous Hanafi Fiqh reference book, and one regarded as a fundamental source in the school, al-Fatawa al-Hindiyya:

> "If a man inserts his penis in his wife's mouth, it is said that it is disliked (makruh), and others said that it is not disliked." (al-Fatawa al-Hindiyya, 5/372)

This clear text from one of the major Hanafi books indicates that the scholars differed on the issue of inserting the penis into the wife's mouth. According to some it was disliked whilst others totally permitted it. But it should be remembered that this is in the case when no sexual fluids enter the spouse's mouth as mentioned in detail earlier. Due to the act being considered against the proper conduct of a Muslim, most scholars have held this practice to be disliked (even in the situation where one does not orally take the filth).

This is what I have on this particular subject. I thought that there was a genuine need to shed some light on it from an Islamic perspective. I hope I have been able to clear the queries people have had on this topic.

And Allah Knows Best

[Mufti] Muhammad ibn Adam

Darul Iftaa

Leicester , UK

Anal Sex with wife

By Shaykh (Mufti) Ebrahim Desai (HA)

Question:I have done anal sex with my husband evev i knew it was haram.is my nikkah break?what should i do?i should get divorce from him?

Answer: In the Name of Allah, Most Compassionate, Most Merciful,

Assalāmu ʿalaykum wa Rahmatullāhi Wabarakātuh

You and your husband should make sincere repentance from this repulsive act and beg Allāh Taʿālā for forgiveness, especially since it was committed knowing well that it was not allowed in the Sharīʿah. In a hadīth of Tirmidhī, the Prophet Salallāhu alaihi wa Sallam stated that Allāh Taʿālā will not even look at the person who commits such an act.

Despite the severity of this sin, the nikāh does not break nor is there a need for divorce. Instead, the husband and wife should make a firm commitment to refrain from this abhorrent act in the future.

And Allāh Taʿāla Knows Best

Wassalāmu ʿalaykum

Ml. Abrar Mirza,
Student Dārul Iftā

Checked and Approved by:
Mufti Ebrahim Desai
Dārul Iftā, Madrasah Inʿāmiyyah

Anal Sex with a Non-Muslim wife

By Shaykh (Mufti) Ebrahim Desai (HA)

Question: I just want to know that i had anal sex with my wife but she is a non Muslim and i am Muslim boy ... tell me what should i do now because i am really worried about that ... and i did nikha with her and after that i heard that the same imam says that you cannot do nikkha with non muslim ... and my wife religion is catholic .. (Christian) please give me the information i really appreciate that Regards

Answer: In the Name of Allah, Most Compassionate, Most Merciful,

Assalāmu ʿalaykum wa Rahmatullāhi Wabarakātuh

To have sexual intercourse in the back passage of a woman is a major sin.

> Rasulullāh Salallāhu alaihi wa Sallam said: "Cursed is the one who has intercourse with his wife in her back passage."[Sunan Abi Da'wud]

Therefore, it is important to make sincere Taubah (repentance) and Istigfār (seeking forgiveness) for committing such an evil act and also to make a firm intention never to return to it.

To marry the Ahle kitāb (people of the book, i.e. Christians and Jews) is permissible. However, one should think of the huge implications of such a marriage.

For example, If the husband is a Muslim, he would have to follow the commands of Almighty Allah by performing Salāh, reading Qurān and abstaining from sin; if he has a wife who is a non Muslim who is used to living a free life of mixing with Ghair mahram men, drinking, eating pork, listening to music and dancing, how then will he be able to fulfil his duties as a Muslims?

More seriously, what would happen when a child is born?

Children by nature follow the ways of their parents; As a Muslim, the father should ensure that his child follows the Deen of Islam, but how would he achieve this when the child is encouraged by its mother to attend church, dress un-Islamic, listen to music and eat pork?

How difficult would it then be for him to steer his children in the right direction?

These are issues that should be carefully thought of before getting married. However, since you have already made nikāh to this lady, it is your duty to present Islam to her and to the best of your ability, encourage her to embrace Islam. May Almighty Allah make this easy for you and guide her to the truth. Ameen.

And Allāh Ta'āla Knows Best

Wassalāmu 'alaykum

Ml. Zakariyya bin Ahmed,
Student Dārul Iftā

Checked and Approved by:
Mufti Ebrahim Desai
Dārul Iftā, Madrasah In'āmiyyah

Practical Steps to help Cure Habit of Masturbation

By Shaykh (Mufti) Muhammad Ibn Adam (HA)

Question: I just wanted some help. I am a 21 year old male and ashamed to say that I have a bad habit of masturbating. I just cannot stop this habit. Would you be able to give me some tips that would help me get rid of this habit?

Answer: In the Name of Allah, Most Compassionate, Most Merciful,

To begin with, it's good to know that you are concerned about this unfortunate practice, Al-Hamdulillah. This is the first step because masturbation is a sin in Islam. May Allah Most High make it easy for you to free yourself from this problem, grant you strength and make you, and all of us, pious and righteous individuals with whom Allah and his beloved Messenger (Allah bless him & give him peace) are pleased, Ameen Ya Rabb!

Masturbation is an extremely unhealthy practice, considered unlawful and sinful in our tradition, which has many personal and societal ill-effects known and recognized by Muslims and many non-Muslims alike. It affects a person in the long-run, ruining one's marriage, impairing one's physical health, reducing one's ability to be proactive in the daily chores, and harming one's religious and spiritual growth by distancing one from one's Lord. Once an addiction is formed to masturbate, the habit continues even after marriage, and in some cases, till one's old age. Masturbation can also lead to psychological impotence. Becoming accustomed to a specific form of sexual gratification, a man will prefer watching porn and satisfying himself instead of having sexual relations with his wife. Hence, this practice must be shunned   immediately.

As for practical ways of getting rid of this habit, I suggest the following:

Take all necessary means to control your sexual desire (shahwa), and avoid anything and everything that may lead you to masturbate. As such:

Guard your gaze against casting it lustfully at women. Avoid going unnecessarily to areas where there is fitna and a greater likelihood of you seeing women dressed immodestly such as shopping malls and town-centers (especially on weekend nights). Try your best in finding alternatives for places of Fitna. For example, use your car to commute rather than a public mode of transport like the underground tube. When travelling abroad, do not wonder around the shops and coffee places at the airport; rather, go and sit in a quiet place and read a book. In the plane, try reading a book or going to sleep instead of looking around and chatting with female air stewardesses. If your work or studies involve being around a lot of women, consider alternatives. See if you can find a job where there is relatively less fitna, and if that is not possible, avoid spending unnecessary time there especially around immodestly dressed females. Make sure to turn your gaze as soon as you see anything inciting such as a billboard advertisement which has immodest images. Completely avoid places where there is casual free mixing of the opposite genders.

Do not watch TV even for news or sports. Avoid surfing the internet unnecessarily, especially when you are alone. When there is a need, try using the internet in a public place or when your family members are around you. In particular, avoid YouTube and other similar sites where there is a greater risk of seeing something Haram.

Always be around family members and other people; try not being alone unless when necessary. Do not sleep alone in your room, and do not have TV or internet to yourself.

Avoid bad company, and endeavor to stay in the company of the pious and righteous, in the Mosque, and with learned Ulama as much as possible.

Try and fast as much as possible, and generally eat less especially foods that may stir your sexual desire such as meat and dairy products.

Continually ask Allah, especially after the Fard prayers, to free you from this habit.

Involve yourself with acts of worship as much as possible, like reciting the Qur'an, Dhikr and Salawat.

Consider marriage. The jurists (fuqaha) state that if one is overwhelmed with sexual desire to the extent that they fear committing a sin, marriage becomes obligatory. Speak to your parents and start looking for a suitable spouse with whom you can fulfill your desires in a Halal way.

Finally, there is nothing more effective in helping you avoid this sinful habit than exercising your will-power (himma) and fighting against your lower, desiring self (nafs) and your sexual appetite. It may be a good idea to impose a monetary or another form of penalty on yourself every time the sin is committed. Continue the struggle wholeheartedly and you will see the benefits, InshaAllah. For more on this, read the books of Imam al-Ghazali (Allah have mercy on him) in particular his *Ihya Ulum al-Din*.

May Allah protect us all, Ameen.

[Mufti] Muhammad ibn Adam

Darul Iftaa

Leicester , UK

Pornography: Why it is Haram & How to deal with it?

Definition of Pornography?

Pornography is defined in the English language as an indecent form of art or literature. Islam also views it as indecent and terms it as faahisha in the Quran.

Allah says (what means): "Say: The things that my Lord has indeed forbidden are: shameful deeds whether open or secret..."

Faahishah is translated as "shameful deeds" because it refers to every bad deed that is noticeably ugly to human beings. In many places in the Quran, Allah (swt) refers to zinaa, adultery and fornication as a faahishah. In another verse, Allah (swt) refers to the marrying of one's father's wife also as being a faahishah because, like adultery, anyone with a pure nature will clearly see it as hideous. Allah (swt) also calls the crime of the people of Lut (as), homosexuality, a faahishah. Likewise to view pictures of nudity, sexual suggestion, intimacy between two people, or a person of the opposite gender who is improperly covered (Islamically) is also an ugly sin to anyone who wishes to adhere to piety.

Television

One of the most pervasive tools of pornography is the television. Shows like "Dawson's Creek" and "Baywatch" have no other purpose except to display blatant degrees of nakedness and indecent scenes of intimacy. Movies also succeed in conveying lewd imagery by almost always including a love/lust story in the story line. However there are other forms of pornography on TV that are much more subtle. For example, most Muslims would not realize that the viewing of several sports events includes pornographic images. The swimsuits that are worn by both men and woman during the Olympics are iniquitously revealing. They expose the 'awrah of a woman and a man for their respective genders and the opposite gender.

129

The word 'awrah refers to those parts of the body which are Islamically prohibited to expose in front of another (either the opposite gender or the same gender). For example, it is a must for a woman to cover all of her body except for her face and hands in front of men who are permissible for her to marry - that is her 'awrah. Likewise the man's 'awrah is everything between his navel and knees while in front of a woman or a man. The skimpy swimsuits worn by these athletes just don't meet the Islamic dress code.

Underwear Ads

Another subtle example regards women who view advertisements that contain pictures of other women modeling bras and underwear. The 'awrah of Muslim women in front of other Muslim women doesn't allow these areas of the body to be exposed and hence it is haram for even a woman to view them.

It is also important to keep in mind that a person could be "clothed but naked" as Rasoolullah (saws) said. For example, competitors in races usually wear some sort of bodysuit that adheres very tightly to their skin and the exact shape of their body parts is apparent. This is almost equivalent to being naked, since it doesn't take much imagination to figure out what is under such type of clothing.

Lowering the Gaze

When such images become prevalent in a society, what is deemed pornographic changes drastically. The very standard of modesty, which should be a defining characteristic of Muslim dress and behavior, will become degraded. The Islamic standard must be upheld. The true believer fears Allah's judgement and knows that no act will go unaccounted for and that even his own eyes will bear witness against him on the Day of Judgement. Allah (swt) says: "Until, when they reach it (Hell-Fire) their hearing and eyes and skin will testify against them as to what they used to do." Rasoolullah (saws) warned us that there is a zinaa of the eyes just as there is a zinaa of the private parts.

The Islamic solution to living in a society where pornographic images are so visible is to lower one's gaze.

Allah (swt) says: "Say to the believing men that they should lower their gaze and guard their modesty: that will make for greater purity for them: and Allah is well aquainted with all they do. And say to the believing women that they should lower their gaze and guard their modesty; that they should not display their beauty and ornaments except what (must ordinarily) appear thereof... "

The scholars of tafseer say that this means that both men and woman are obliged to direct their sight away from that which is haram and that there is no harm in looking at that which is halal (such as viewing one's spouse while they are uncovered).

In regard to these verses Ibn al-Qayyim (rahimahullah) says: "So He (Allah) put purity after lowering of the gaze and protecting of the private parts. For this reason lowering the gaze away from the prohibited things warrants three great benefits. The first of them is the sweetness of Imaan and the pleasure that comes from it, which is more sweet and pleasing than that which he diverted his eyes away from for Allah's sake. Verily, whoever abandons a thing for Allah's sake, He (swt) compensates him with better than it...The second benefit is a light in the heart and quality of intuition... and the third benefit is the strength of the heart and steadfastness and courage. So Allah (swt) would give him, by His strength, the ability of wisdom and substantiation, and the devil would flee from him as it has been mentioned in the saying, "Whoever fears his whims, the devil would race out of his shadow."

Indeed, the opposite is also true. This is because the eyes are the most direct path to the heart. One who allows his whims to overwhelm him and indulges his eyes in the viewing of haram things has weakened his heart, corrupted his soul, and invited shaytan to control him.

Why is Pornography Haram?

"I just found out that at least one of my sons spent some time this afternoon (signed on as me) going to XXX rated (web) sites. They are 13 and 11. I am so upset, I do not know what to do. Insha Allah, it is a curiosity thing, but I am totally blown away by this." (A mother in Sound Vision's parenting forum)

Internet pornography is the latest media menace parents and anyone concerned about children and morality in general, must deal with. Pictures of naked women (its usually women, since most pornography caters to heterosexual men) and couples engaged in various forms of sexual intercourse, to name just a few of the contents of pornography, are not just reserved to the internet though.

For decades, 'porn' in various forms has been found in magazines, films, and more recently during a lot of prime time television.

The Internet is just the latest tool pornographers have found to spread their "art," which poses a number of problems.

The pervasiveness of pornography on the Internet means Muslims need to consider once again the Islamic perspective on this issue while they use this new medium.

The Islamic Perspective:

"There is no room for anyone to say pornography is not Haram. It's ab solutely Haram," notes Shaykh Muhammad Nur Abdullah. He is the Imam of the Islamic Foundation of Greater St. Louis in Missouri.

"If someone is looking at someone committing Zina (sex outside of marriage) whether it is movies or pictures or the actual thing, it is all Haram," he adds. Some of the proofs he gives for the prohibition of pornography in Islam include verses 30 and 31 of chapter 24 (Noor) of the Qur'an, as well as Ahadith that say what leads to Haram is Haram and that Zina is committed by the eye and the hand, even before a sexual encounter takes place.

He has openly discussed the problem of the Internet, pornography and Muslim youth in his Khutbahs. On a day to day level, he says he gets at least two cases daily of young Muslims, boys and girls, who come to the mosque and speak to him personally about this problem.

Dremali says the teenagers feel guilty, but they cannot stop looking at this material. They need a cure, they have become addicted.

"The person who looks at these things will always have Shaytan in his mind because he wants to commit these [actions]," he says. "Shaytan never takes the person immediately to commit adultery (he does it in steps)."

132

Dremali also gives a clear example of the role the Internet plays in being one of the steps leading to sex outside of marriage.

"The hand commits adultery by touching Haram and the person using the keyboard and using the mouse to look at these pictures, he or she is committing adultery," he warns

"Unfortunately there are a lot of Muslim youth who are using pornography on the [Internet], and they basically use the Internet only for that purpose," notes Taha Ghayyur, 19, who is National Coordinator of Young Muslims Canada.

Too often, though, parents are willing to bury their heads in the sand when the issue of pornography and their children comes up. "How do you know your kids don't know about it?" asks Dremali.

The easy access to pornography on television (no longer reserved to just the very late night hours), on the magazine stands and the Internet makes it almost impossible to avoid, even if one's intentions are clear.

In the case of the Internet, sometimes accompanying links or windows to pornographic websites or WebPages will suddenly open up, against the wishes of the surfer.

This however, does not mean parents should automatically assume the worst about their children.

Shaykh Nur Abdullah stresses the importance of openly talking to children about the problem, especially if they have been caught looking at such material. If parents don't do this "then we are turning our face away from the problem," he says.

"[the] Internet is good and bad," says Dremali. "Allah gave us the brains to think where is the good way and where is the bad way. According to your choice Allah will judge you.

Some Statistics and Facts on Pornography:

Over 30% of sites on the World Wide Web are pornographic" (USA Today).

Looking for one thing, finding another:

"Our Internet search engine reports reveal a disturbing reality. In over 99% of the hits directed to our site, the person performing the search was looking for pornography, many looking for child pornography. To think, 99% used pornography search words inspired our project, Internet Intervention. Internet Intervention is a network of computers, hosting hundreds of websites, which direct the keyword searcher of child pornography to an Intervention Help Site. The very people that need it the most see our message of help. Click here to see a help website that you could have been directed to if you use child pornography search words on your search engine request." (From the website of the Tonya Flynt Foundation, an anti-pornography website. Tony Flynt is the daughter of notorious American pornographer Larry Flynt)

A MULTI BILLION DOLLAR INDUSTRY:

Pornography is a $12-$13 billion- a-year industry - more than the combined annual revenues of the Coca-Cola and McDonnell Douglas corporations. (From an Affair of the Mind by Laurie Hall)

Pornographic entertainment on the Internet constituted the third largest sector of sales in cyberspace, with estimated annual revenues of $100 million. Such marketing success has fueled an increase in the size of the pornography industry -- $10 billion annually, according to conservative estimates. (Anthony Flint, Skin Trade Spreading Across U.S., Boston Sunday Globe)

HITS ON A PORN SITE:

Playboy's headquarters received 4.7 million hits (electronic visits) in a recent seven day period. (Promise Keepers website)

PORN VIDEO RENTALS:

Porn video rentals soared to 665 million in 1996, accounting for 13.3% of video rentals in America. Profits of sales and rentals of porn videos was $4.2 billion in 1996. (USA Today, & UPI News)

ADDICTION TO PORNOGRAPHY:

Pornography consumption can be as "mood altering" and as addictive as narcotics. (A study by Richard Drake, assistant professor at Brigham Young University College of Nursing).

Studies show pornography is progressive and addictive for many. It often leads to the user acting out his fantasy often on children. (Victor Cline, Ph.D., Department of Psychology, University of Utah, Pornography Effects: Empirical and Clinical Evidence, pg. 24)

PORNOGRAPHY AND SEX ADDICTION:

The average age of first time contact of pornography among sex addicts is 11. (American Family Association Outreach)

PORNOGRAPHY'S EFFECTS ON FATHERS:

More sophisticated analysis reveals that men who had "purchased pornographic materials in the past year" had significantly lower marital, fathering and family-life satisfaction when compared to those who had not purchased pornographic materials in the past year. (National Center for Fathering)

PORNOGRAPHY AND SEXUAL ASSAULT:

Research gathered over the past few decades demonstrates that pornography contributes to sexual assault, including rape and the molestation of children. (Pornography Victims Compensation Act of 1992, U.S. Senate Comm. on the Judiciary)

Child molesters often use pornography to seduce their prey, to lower the inhibitions of the victim, and to serve as an instrnction manual. (W.L. Marshall, Ph.D., Pornography and Sexual Offenders, in Pornography: Research Advances and Policy)

WHO CONSUMES PORNOGRAPHY:

A primary pornography consumer group is boys between ages 12 - 17.9 (Attorney General's Final Report on Pornography)

PORNOGRAPHY'S EFFECT ON SEXUAL RELATIONSHIPS:

Pornography distorts the natural development of personality. If the early stimulus is pornographic photographs, the adolescent can be conditioned to become aroused through photographs. Once this pairing is rewarded a number of times, it is likely to become permanent. The result to the individual is that it becomes difficult for the person to seek out relations with appropriate persons. (Jerry Bergman, Ph.D., The Influence of Pornography on Sexual Development: Three Case Histories, IX Family Therapy)

Pornography Addiction

By Ustadha Zaynab Ansari (HA)

Question: I have a pornography problem. I am 16 years old and when I am finished pleasing myself I often feel guilty and disgusted by myself and what I become at times for those couple of minutes. And now I have noticed that I am viewing gay porn instead. I know everything that I am doing is wrong and completely forbidden. I have started to stop myself but it is hard. I mean I don't want to continue this habit of masturbating and watching porn, or even the factor of me being gay to come into play. I have been going to the mosque regularly and I have tried to increase my iman. I feel when I enter the mosque that I am secured and away from all things bad?

Answer: In the Name of Allah, Most Compassionate, Most Merciful,

I pray this message reaches you in good health and spirits.

My teachers caution against looking at images, even those which may be permissible, simply because of the effect they can have on one's heart, and the way they can be a door to the unlawful. It's amazing (and sad) how seemingly innocent web surfing can deteriorate into time wasting, which, in turn can degenerate into the haram.

Here are some tips, which may or may not be helpful. Ultimately, Allah Most High is the only one who can assist you in subduing the lower self, which calls you to these sinful things. So please seek Allah's guidance. Implore Him to give you an exit from these unlawful habits.

Once the door of pornography is opened, it is very hard to close. You will have to be firm with yourself, even unyielding, if you want to put an end to this habit. Shut the door to temptation by getting rid of your computer. This may sound drastic, but it is helpful to put this instrument out of your life, until such time you can use it for the good of your soul. If you can't get rid of it, at the very least change out your hard drive and memory.

Look at how and when you use your computer and drastically change these habits. If you get online in private, then, from now on, only use the computer when others are around. If you look at these things at night, then refrain from turning the computer on altogether during these hours.

By looking at porn, you are willingly putting yourself in a situation in which you will consistently feel temporary, yet completely false, gratification. The problem with this type of "instant" gratification is that it leaves you empty, broken, guilty, and self-loathing. Why put yourself through this? True gratification only comes when you enjoy sexual activity through lawful means, that is, with a spouse. Anything else simply harms your heart and soul.

Finally, and most importantly, you must take steps toward sincere repentance. Sincere repentance consists of :

Turning away from the sin

Feeling remorse

Resolving to never go back

Changing one's environment so that the temptation is removed

Please avail yourself of the beautiful literature on repentance. There are many Qur'anic verses and Prophetic traditions on repentance.

Allah Most High, says,

> "Say: "O my Servants who have transgressed against their souls! Despair not of the Mercy of Allah. for Allah forgives all sins: for He is Oft-Forgiving, Most Merciful.Turn ye to our Lord (in repentance) and bow to His (Will), before the Penalty comes on you: after that ye shall not be helped" (Az-Zumar, 39:53-54).
>
> And the Prophet, Allah bless him and give him peace, said, "Allah the Mighty and Majestic accepts the repentance of His servant as long as long as his death-rattle has not begun" [At-Tirmidhi, Riyad al-Salihin]

Cultivate good habits, and Allah willing, these will replace the bad ones. Establish a connection with the Book of Allah by reading it and reflecting on it daily. Contemplate the noble example of the Prophet, Allah bless him and give him peace, and the biographies of his companions, Allah be pleased with them, to see how you can implement these life lessons.

And, find good Muslim friends. This is of huge importance in fortifying yourself against temptation.

May Allah Ta'ala make things easy for you.

Custody of Children after divorce

When a husband files for a legal divorce, he appoints the court to divorce his wife on his behalf. Islamically, a husband has a right to divorce his wife either himself or by appointing someone else as his representative to divorce his wife on his behalf. It is not necessary that this 'representative' be a Muslim, as is the case in filing/petitioning for a legal divorce through the courts.

Child Custody after Divorce

By Shaykh (Mufti) Muhammad Ibn Adam (HA)

Question:

What are the Islamic duties of a father, if he divorces or separates from the wife, who has a child?

Who has the right to the child, the father or mother?

Who is responsible for the financial responsibility of the child? When they are divorced?

What are the responsibilities or duties of the father, when he divorces is wife and she takes the child. And he gets married to another woman. And his divorced wife stays single or gets married. Does the father forget his child from his previous marriage and carry on with his new life and family or must he visit and keep contact with his child in his   previous   marriage?

Basically these are some of the key questions I need to ask,

but can you address what the Islamic Shariah says about these matters, 'about when the husband divorces or separates form his wife and they have a child and everything related to that'. The father's role in the future of his child from his previous marriage?

Answer: In the Name of Allah, Most Compassionate, Most Merciful,

I f and when a marriage unfortunately comes to an end, the problems of the parties involved should not in any way affect the children. Children are a trust (amanah) from Allah Most High and they should be treated and looked after in a proper manner.

They have many rights, of which two are of utmost importance: to receive proper care and love, and the other proper upbringing (tarbiyah). These rights of a child can not be fulfilled except with the joint endeavour of the parents. The love, care and attention of the mother is just as important as the upbringing and training of the father.

In light of the above, divorce should definitely be avoided as much as possible, especially in the case where there are children involved. The Messenger of Allah (Allah bless him & give him peace) said:

"Divorce is the most hated of all lawful (halal) things in the sight of Allah." (Sunan Abu Dawud, no. 2178)

However, if divorce did take place, and both parties demand their rights, then the right of custody will be in the following way. In should be remembered here that there is nothing wrong in making a mutual arrangement, as long as there is no objection from those who have a right to custody:

The mother has a right of custody for a male child until the child is capable of taking care of his own basic bodily functions and needs, such as eating, dressing and cleaning himself. This has been recognized at seven years of age.

Imam al-Haskafi (Allah have mercy on him) states:

"The custody of a male child is the right of the mother until the child is capable of taking care of his own self. This has been approximated at seven years of age, and the Fatwa (legal verdict) has been issued on this age, as normally children are able to take care of themselves at this age." (See: Radd al-Muhtar, 3/566)

In the case of a female, the mother has this right of custody until she reaches puberty. This has been declared at nine years of age. (al-Mawsili, al-Ikhtiyar li ta'lil al-mukhtar, 3/237)

The right of custody will be taken away from the mother if she:

Leaves Islam,

Openly indulges in sins such as adultery and there is a fear of the child being affected,

She does not attend to the child due to her leaving the house very often,

She marries a non-relative (stranger) to the child by which the child may be affected,

She demands payment for the upbringing of the child if there is another woman to raise the child without remuneration.

In the above cases (when the mother no longer has the right to custody), this right then transfers to the following, in order:

Maternal grandmother, and on up;

Paternal grandmother, and on up;

Full sisters,

Maternal half sisters,

Paternal half sisters,

Maternal aunts,

Paternal aunts,

After all the avenues of the female have been exhausted as explained by the Jurists, the males have the right of custody in the following sequence:

Father,

Paternal grandfather,

Real brother,

Paternal brother,

Maternal brother,

The reason for this is that, in the early years, the mother and the other female relatives are more suitable for raising the young child (regardless of sex) with love, mercy, attention, and motherly care. The male child after reaching the age of understanding (7) is in need of education and acquiring masculine traits, which is why he is then transferred to the father. The female child, after reaching the age of understanding is in need of being inculcated with female traits, which she receives by living with her mother. After reaching puberty, she is in need of protection which the father offers.

In a Hadith recorded by Imam Abu Dawud in his Sunan, the Messenger of Allah (Allah bless him & give him peace) said to a woman who complained that her husband was intending to take her child away from her:

"You are more rightful of the child as long as you don't marry." (Sunan Abu Dawud, no. 2276 & Mustadrak al-Hakim, 2/207)

It should also be remembered that after the transferral of custody from the mother to the father, the boy remains in the custody of the father until puberty, at which point, if he is mature and wise, he is free to choose with whom to live, or to live on his own. As for the girl, custody remains with the father until she marries. (See: Qadri pasha, Hanafi articles, 498 & 499)

Irrespective of who (mother/father) has the right of custody, the other party has visitation rights according to mutual understanding and consent. Generally, the party having the rights of custody use the child as a weapon to punish the other party by depriving them of visitation rights. This is totally against the concept of Islam and a severe, brutal and grave sin indeed, and also very harmful to the child. Unfortunately, many so called "religious" people are also involved in this heinous act.

At all times, the father of the child is responsible for maintaining the child; in the case of a female, until she marries; while in the case of a healthy male, until he reaches maturity. In the case of a disabled child (male or female) the father is permanently responsible.

When the mother has the rights of custody but does not have a shelter to stay in with the child, the father must provide shelter for both. (See: Radd al-Muhtar of Ibn Abidin).

With the above, I hope all your questions have been answered.

And Allah Knows Best

[Mufti] Muhammad ibn Adam

Darul Iftaa

Leicester , UK

Can my Ex-Wife move to another Country with my Child?

By Shaykh (Mufti) Muhammad Ibn Adam (HA)

Question: I live in England and my ex-wife is from Toronto, Canada. Unfortunately, we recently underwent a divorce. She left England with our child to her home country without my permission. I am not able to provide my child with any support, care and security. I am unable to take care of his proper upbringing, schooling, and other guardianship duties. I tried moving there for the sake of my child but I can not move to that country myself because I am not allowed to work there.

If she moves here, I can provide her with living. But while she is there, and my son is raised there, he will be deprived of fatherly care and guardianship. I want to know whether Islamically she is allowed to remain there without my permission. Can she let the child forgo his fatherhood care, security and support just

because his mother wants to live and raise him in her home country?

Answer: In the Name of Allah, Most Compassionate, Most Merciful,

As explained in previous answers, the mother has a right of custody over a male child until he is capable of taking care of his own basic bodily functions and needs such as eating, dressing, and cleansing himself. This has been determined at seven (Islamic) years of age, since children are normally able to take care of themselves at this age.

From the age of seven Islamic years till he attains puberty, the father has a right of custody over him. After puberty, the boy, if he is mature and wise, can choose to live with whosoever he wishes, or live on his own.

In the case of a female child, the mother has a right of custody over her until she reaches the age of puberty (i.e. she starts menstruating). This has been approximated at nine (Islamic) years of age. Thereafter, the father has a right of custody over her until she marries. (Ibn Abidin, Radd al-Muhtar ala 'l-Durr al-Mukhtar 3/566, Qadri Basha, Hanafi articles 498 & 499 & al-Mawsili, al-Ikhtiyar li ta'lil al-Mukhtar 3/237)

It was also explained previously that irrespective of who from the mother and father has custody-rights, the other party is entitled to the right of visitation according to mutual understanding and agreement. It is unlawful and a grave sin to deprive the other party of their visitation right.

In view of this very reason, and also in view of the fact that the father is responsible for the proper upbringing (tarbiya) and financial maintenance of the child, the jurists (fuqaha) have outlined rules in regards to whether the mother (during her period of custody) is allowed to move with the child to another region or not.

After a lengthy and somewhat tiresome discussion on the subject by Hanafi Imams: Tumurtashi, Haskafi and Ibn Abidin (may Allah have mercy on them all) in Radd al-Muhtar ala 'l-Durr al-Mukhtar Sharh Tanwir al-Absar, Imam Ibn Abidin himself summarized the juristic ruling with the following:

"In clear and concise terms it could be said: A divorced woman is permitted to move (khuruj) with the child from a village to a nearby town/city, but not vice versa (i.e. from a town/city to a nearby village). And [she is permitted to move with the child] from one city to another city provided it is her hometown and he (the father of the child) had contracted marriage with her there..." (Radd al-Muhtar 3/570)

A few lines prior to the above text, he states:

"Two conditions are indispensable for the permissibility of [the mother of the child] moving to a distant city: It being her hometown, and the marriage being contracted there." (Ibid)

Likewise, Shaykh Muhammad Qudri Basha explains in his standard codification of Hanafi personal law, al-Akham al-Shar'iyya fi 'l-Ahwal al-Shakhsiyya that the mother is not allowed to move with the child without the father's permission to a distant town/city, unless it is her hometown and he married her there, in which case she is permitted to move there without his consent, even if the town/city is distant from the father's place of residence.

He further states that if where she intends to move is her hometown but the marriage was not contracted there, or the marriage was contracted there but it is not her hometown, then in both cases, she is not permitted to move there with the child without the child's father's permission, unless the place is nearby to the residence of the father in a manner that he is able to visit his child and return home before night. (See: al-Akham al-Shar'iyya fi 'l-Ahwal al-Shakhsiyya, Item no 393)

So, in view of these texts of the Hanafi School, we may conclude by saying that if the (divorced) mother, during her period of custody, wants to move with the child to a nearby city or town where the child's father is able to come, visit the child, and return home before night-time, she can do so without the father's permission in all situations. If, however, she desires to move to a distant city or town where the child's father is not able to come, visit the child, and return home before night-time, then she can only do so provided it is her hometown and provided her marriage with the child's father was contracted there.

As such, if Toronto is your ex-wife's hometown and your marriage to her was contracted there, then she is free to move there with your child without your consent. However, such issues are best resolved through mutual understanding, regard for one another, tact, love, and keeping the child's interests in mind. If she does decide to move there with your child, both of you should try and come to some sort of mutual arrangement where the child is sent to live with you for some time during the year, for example.

And Allah Knows Best

[Mufti] Muhammad ibn Adam

Darul Iftaa

Leicester , UK

Court (Civil) Divorce

When a husband files for a legal divorce, he appoints the court to divorce his wife on his behalf. Islamically, a husband has a right to divorce his wife either himself or by appointing someone else as his representative to divorce his wife on his behalf. It is not necessary that this 'representative' be a Muslim, as is the case in filing/petitioning for a legal divorce through the courts.

Legal Divorce According to Islamic Law

By Shaykh (Mufti) Muhammad Ibn Adam (HA)

Question: I have a question about Islamic Divorce that I hope you can help me with.

I just wanted to know if I as a husband file for a legal and civil divorce here in the UK courts, would that automatically count as an Islamic divorce, or would I have to give a separate Islamic divorce. Please explain?

Answer: In the Name of Allah, Most Compassionate, Most Merciful,

According to Shariah, speech and verbal utterance is not a necessary condition for the validity of a divorce (talaq). Rather, divorce is also effected by means of the written word.

The great Hanafi jurist, Imam al-Kasani (Allah have mercy on him) states:

"Issuing a divorce verbally is not a condition. Hence, divorce will come into effetc with clear and unambiguous writing, or with the understood gesture of a dumb person, for the clear written word is in place of verbal utterance." (Bada'i al-Sana'i, 3/100)

This writing must be clear and unambiguous. It must be written out of one's own will and not be forced. Also, there should be no deception in getting the husband to write out the decree of divorce.

Moreover, if a husband instructs a third person - even if a non-Muslim - to write the decree of divorce on his behalf and he then signs the written document, or he appoints a third parson to issue divorce on his behalf (tawkil), divorce will come into effect.

Imam Ibn Abidin (Allah have mercy on him) states:

"If the husband requested another person to write the declaration of divorce for him, and he (the writer) after writing it, read it out to the husband who took the divorce paper, signed and stamped it, and sent it to his wife, divorce will be effected if the husband admits that it is his writing." (Radd al-Muhtar, 3/246-247)

Shaykh Qadri Pasha explains, in his decisive codification of Hanafi personal law, Al-Ahkam al-Shar'iyya fi'l Ahwal al-Shakhsiyya, which is a primary source for the personal law of several Muslim countries, and continues to be taught and used across the Islamic world:

"(Item 222) Divorce may be affected in speech or in clear, understandable writing, whether signed by the husband or someone he has given agency to do so on his behalf..."

Taking the above into consideration:

If a husband files for a legal divorce, he in theory is appointing the court as his agent to divorce his wife. As such, when the court issues the Absolute Decree of divorce, it constitutes an Islamic divorce also - resulting in one irrevocable (ba'in) divorce.

Appointing a non-Muslim an agent is considered valid in Shari'ah. (See: Radd al-Muhtar).

If a wife petitions/files for a legal divorce, and the husband – understanding the contents of the divorce papers sent to him – signs and gives his 'clear' and 'absolute' consent for the divorce to go ahead, then this too constitutes an Islamic Divorce, when the Decree Absolute is issued by the court.

However, if the husband does not sign on any written document or he fails to give his 'clear' consent for the court to go ahead with the divorce, but the court divorces him on behalf of his wife against his will, then this does not constitute a valid Islamic divorce.

Therefore, in your situation, if you filed for the divorce or gave your full consent and signed on the legal divorce papers, then you have divorced your wife from an Islamic perspective also. There is no need to go through some other form of Islamic procedure of divorce.

And Allah Knows Best

[Mufti] Muhammad ibn Adam

Darul Iftaa

Leicester , UK

Made in the USA
Monee, IL
07 August 2023

40613489R00085